921
92-29

D0093723

HAFIZ
AL-ASAD
OF SYRIA

IN FOCUS

HAFIZ
AL-ASAD
OF SYRIA

CHARLES PATTERSON

For Marilyn

Published by Julian Messner, a division of
Silver Burdett Press, Inc., Simon & Schuster, Inc.
Prentice Hall Bldg., Englewood Cliffs, NJ 07632

JULIAN MESSNER and colophon are trademarks of
Simon & Schuster, Inc. Design by Leslie Bauman.
Manufactured in the United States of America.

Lib. ed.   10 9 8 7 6 5 4 3 2 1
Paper ed.   10 9 8 7 6 5 4 3 2 1

Library of Congress Cataloging-in-Publication Data
Patterson, Charles.
Hafiz al-Asad of Syria / Charles Patterson.
p.   cm.—(In focus biographies)
Includes bibliographical references and index.
Summary: Describes the childhood, rise to power, and political
influence of the military leader who has been president of Syria
since 1970.
1. Asad, Hafiz, 1928—Juvenile literature.   2. Presidents—
Syria—Biography—Juvenile literature. 3. Syria—Politics and
government—Juvenile literature. [1. Asad, Hafiz, 1928
2. Presidents—Syria. 3. Syria—Politics and government.]
I. Title.   II. Series.
DS98.3.A8P38   1991
956.9104'2'092—dc20
[B]
[92]   ISBN 0-671-69469-3 (paper ed.)   90-40243
ISBN 0-671-69468-5 (lib. ed)   CIP
AC

ISBN 0-671-69468-5 LSB
ISBN 0-671-69469-3 paper

CONTENTS

ASAD AND SYRIA

I n 1974 when President Nixon met Hafiz al-Asad in Damascus, he found him to have "a great deal of mystique, tremendous stamina, and a lot of charm." Nixon was clearly impressed by the Syrian president. "All in all," said Nixon, "he is a man of real substance, and at his age—44—if he can avoid somebody shooting him or overthrowing him, he will be a leader to be reckoned with in this part of the world."[1]

After two decades of rule, President Hafiz al-Asad of Syria certainly has made himself into a leader to be reckoned with. He has been in power longer than most world leaders and far longer than anybody else in the history of modern Syria. Since the coup that put him in power in 1970, Asad has turned Syria into a powerful force in the Middle East.

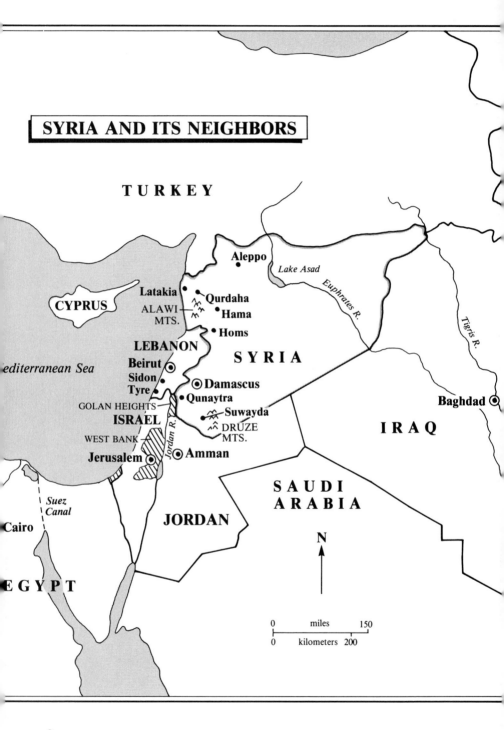

SYRIA AND ITS NEIGHBORS

TURKEY

Aleppo

Lake Asad

Latakia
Qurdaha
ALAWI
MTS.
Hama

Homs

CYPRUS

Euphrates R.

Tigris R.

SYRIA

LEBANON

editerranean Sea

Beirut
Sidon
Tyre

Damascus

Qunaytra

Baghdad

GOLAN HEIGHTS

Suwayda
DRUZE
MTS.

ISRAEL

I R A Q

WEST BANK

Jordan R.

Jerusalem

Amman

**S A U D I
A R A B I A**

*Suez
Canal*

N

Cairo

JORDAN

E G Y P T

0	miles	150
0	kilometers	200

Today Asad is the leader of the Arab struggle against Israel and the dominant power in Lebanon. Since he has succeeded in placing himself at the center of events in the region, there is little chance that there could ever be a peaceful settlement to the Arab-Israeli conflict without him. More than any other world leader, President Asad holds in his hand the key to the future of the Middle East.

SYRIA—AN OVERVIEW

The country over which Asad rules is a land of variety and contrast. Located at the eastern end of the Mediterranean Sea, Syria has several distinct regions. Each has its own scenery and climate. The narrow coastal area, which stretches for about 110 miles from Turkey to Lebanon, has a rich soil that is watered by springs and plentiful rainfall. Since crops grow all year round along the coast, the region is densely settled and cultivated.

Farther inland are mountain ranges that run parallel to the coast and extend down into southern Syria. The winds blow in off the sea and deposit up to 40 inches of rain a year on the western slopes of these ranges. The farming is better there than on the drier eastern slopes. The small village where Asad grew up is on the western slope of the Alawi mountains.

To the east of the mountains lies the central Syrian plain. In this region are the country's major cities—Aleppo, Hama, Homs, and the Syrian capital, Damascus. The central plain has low rainfall, a dry atmosphere, and hot days. However, extensive irrigation has made it possible to grow crops throughout the area.

Farther east lies the Syrian desert. This region consists mostly of dry steppes and grasslands where nomads graze their flocks. It has few natural resources, with the notable exception of the Euphrates River, which crosses eastern Syria from northwest to southeast. The river and its tributaries provide power and irrigate the soil for the growing of cotton, grain, and fruits. The Euphrates River is the country's most important water source.

An Arab village in the Syrian desert. Note the beehive-shaped buildings.

Today the Syrian economy is more balanced than that of just about any other Arab country. Although the government controls much of the economy, most farms, light industries, small businesses, and retail trade are in private hands. A half a century ago Syria hardly had any industry. However, since its independence Syria has made great progress in manufacturing, mining, and commerce.

In the 1970s Asad embarked on a policy of rapid industrialization that gave priority to heavy industries, such as oil, chemicals, iron, steel, cement, and fertilizers. Asad's government also built a national transportation network of railways, roads, and ports that expanded the country's industrial capacity. Today Syrian industry employs about a fifth of all Syrian workers and accounts for about a fourth of the value of goods and services.

However, agriculture is still by far the largest part of the Syrian economy. About half the country's workers are employed in farming, which provides about a fifth of the value of all goods and services produced in Syria. Cotton and wheat are Syria's main crops. Farmers also grow barley, tobacco, sugar beets, grapes, olives, onions, and tomatoes.

HISTORY

Although it has been independent only since the end of World War II, Syria has an ancient history. Throughout its long history, Syria covered an area very much larger than what Syria covers today. Until 1918, Greater Syria, as it was called, included much of what is today Lebanon, Jordan, Israel, and parts of Turkey.

Syria was the cradle of some of the world's oldest civilizations. However, Syria's location on major trade and military routes linking Africa, Asia, and Europe made it vulnerable to conquest and rule by foreigners. Among these foreign rulers were Assyrians, Babylonians, Egyptians, Persians, Greeks, Romans, and Byzantine Christians.

Then, in the seventh century, Syria's history took a dramatic turn. Armies from the Arabian Peninsula, aflame with a new religion started by Muhammad, conquered the Middle East, North Africa, and Spain. These Muslim Arab invaders converted Syria to Islam and Arab ways. For one brief, shining moment under the Umayyad caliphate (A.D. 661–750) Syria was the center of the Islamic world.

Syria's moment ended when the Abbasids in neighboring Iraq took over the leadership of the Islamic world and ruled it from their capital, Baghdad. In the centuries that followed, Syria fell under the domination of another series of foreign rulers—Turks, Crusaders, Mongols, Egyptian Mamelukes, and Ottoman Turks.

The Ottoman Turkish Empire annexed Syria in 1516 and, except for one brief interruption, ruled it for the next four centuries. The Ottoman Turks divided Syria up into provinces and ruled them through Syrian intermediaries—tribal sheiks, clan leaders, religious dignitaries, and wealthy landowners. The Turkish policy of

Ruins of the Temple of the Sun at Palmyra. Located in central Syria, the ancient city of Palmyra was an important trading center. It became a nearly self-ruling state in the 3rd century A.D. but was eventually destroyed by the Romans, who feared its power.

using local leaders to collect taxes and keep order made a small number of Syrian families powerful and wealthy at the expense of everybody else. Syrians resented that Turks collected taxes but did not bother to provide services like roads, schools, and health care.

After World War I (1914–1918) the victors, France and Britain, secretly agreed to divide up the provinces of the defeated Ottoman Empire. France took the northern part of the Ottoman provinces, which later became Syria and Lebanon. Britain took the southern part, which became Palestine (later Israel) and Transjordan. In 1920 the League of Nations voted to give to the French and British mandates, or the right to rule, over the entire area.

Syrians resented the way France went on to carve Syria up into separate parts. The French took the large coastal area of southern Syria called Lebanon, where their Christian allies lived, and separated it from the rest of Syria. The French also gave parts of northern Syria to Turkey. By the time France finally pulled out of Syria in 1946, Syria had been stripped of more than a third of its land.

The French divided the rest of Syria up into four separate parts. These parts consisted of two large states, with Damascus and Aleppo as their capitals, and two small mountain states for the Druzes and the Alawites (the Syrian minority to which Asad belongs). Syrian nationalists resented this French policy of divide and rule.

After Syria finally achieved its independence and France withdrew its troops in 1946, many Syrians still had dreams of a reunited Greater Syria. In 1948, when the United Nations divided part of Greater Syria—Palestine—into a Jewish state (Israel) and an Arab state, Syria joined other Arab states in a war against the newly created state of Israel. After the Arab failure to defeat the Israelis, Syrians blamed their government. In 1949 alone there were no less than three military coups. For the next 20 years there were many more until Asad seized power in 1970 and put an end to the frequent changes of government.

ALAWITES

Syria has a variety of peoples. The majority (70 percent) are Sunni Muslims. But there are also Shiite Muslims, Alawites, Druzes, and Ismailis, as well as assorted non-Muslims—Christians, Jews, Turks, Kurds, Armenians, Circassians, and Assyrians. The official language of Syria is Arabic, which most Syrians speak. French, Kurdish, Armenian, and English are also spoken.

Asad and his family belong to the Alawites, who make up 12 percent of the Syrian population. Alawite, or Alawi, means "a follower of Ali." Ali was the Prophet Muhammad's cousin and son-in-law. Like Shiite Muslims, Alawites believe Ali was the rightful heir of Muhammad and was cheated out of his inheritance by the early caliphs, or Muslim rulers.

When the Sunni Muslims established their dominance in the Arab world in the twelfth century, they denounced Shiites and other offshoot groups like the Alawites as heretics. Persecuted and threatened with death by the Sunni majority, Alawites and other Shiite groups had to flee for their lives to remote areas where they could live in safety and practice their own beliefs. Alawites came originally from Arabia, but persecutions drove them farther and farther west until they ended up in the Alawi mountains in western Syria. There, through stubborn persistence, they have survived for centuries in the face of persecutions. Even the Ottoman Turks tried to force the Alawites to accept Sunni Muslim beliefs, but they failed.

The Alawites did not experience a measure of freedom from persecution until the French granted them their own mini-state after World War I. Many Alawites hoped the special character of the Alawite state would be preserved after the French left Syria, but they were disappointed. The new Syrian government in Damascus sent troops up into the Alawi mountain villages to subdue Alawite separatists and bring the Alawites into the new nation of Syria.

Alawites would rarely venture down into the rest of Syria, where they were despised and made to feel like outsiders. However, French encouragement of Alawite separatism did give the Alawites more pride and self-confidence. Some Alawite families moved down from their mountain villages to Latakia on the coast to find work and improve their lives.

During the French mandate, many poor Alawite young men joined the French defense force used to put down uprisings in other parts of Syria. Although the French did introduce elementary education into mountain villages, they did little to improve Alawite living standards. Under the French, villages like the one Asad grew up in remained poor and backward. A British officer who visited

Asad and his wife Aniseh and their young children.

several Alawite villages during the French mandate observed: "The wretched inhabitants were in a deplorable state of misery, dejection, and abandon ... the conditions everywhere were unbelievably bad."[2]

ASAD THE MAN

Asad dislikes crowds and rarely appears in public, but Syrians are never allowed to forget that he is their ruler. His picture is everywhere. When he reviews Syrian troops or meets with an important foreign visitor, radio microphones and television cameras are there to record the occasion and transmit the words and images to the Syrian people. Yet few Syrians ever see their leader in person because Asad is private and secretive by nature. Asad lives behind a shield of tight security that protects him and his government.

Asad, his wife, and their grown children. All of Asad's children attended Damascus University.

Asad guards his family's privacy zealously as well. Asad and his wife have been married since 1958, but she appears in public only once a year. Occasionally, however, she is seen at her husband's side when a foreign dignitary visits Syria with his wife. Asad and his wife have five children. After growing up behind the tight security that protected their life at home, all five children attended Damascus University. There they set a good example by working hard and behaving in a way that reflected well on their father. Asad's oldest child and only daughter, named Bushra after Asad's firstborn who died in infancy, studied pharmacology. Asad's four sons—Basil, Bashar, Mahir, and Majd—studied civil engineering, medicine, business, and electrical engineering, respectively.

While they were growing up, the children saw little of their father. A compulsively hard worker, Asad worked at least 14 hours a day and rarely slept. Nor did he take time off for vacations or holidays. He rarely had time to eat meals with his children, and during crises he would often go days at a time without seeing them. In spite of his frequent absences, his children are said to respect their father and remain devoted and loyal.

Asad has made many enemies through the years. Although the last major threat to his rule was crushed in 1982, he needs to be constantly on the alert. He has many critics at home and abroad, especially in Paris where many Syrian exiles live. Inside Syria there are many who complain, but because of the effectiveness of his security forces, there is little active resistance. After a long fight, Asad made it to the summit of political power in Syria in 1970. Alone at the top, he has been there ever since.

SOURCES—CHAPTER 1

[1]Ma'oz, *Asad*, p. 100
[2]Seale, *Asad*, p. 22

CHILDHOOD

The small village of Qurdaha where Asad grew up and his family lived for generations is located on the western slope of the Alawi Mountains in northwestern Syria, not far from the Mediterranean Sea. The village has a healthful climate, with an annual rainfall of about 30 inches. Qurdaha's two main crops are olives and tobacco. Olives provide the oil for cooking, lighting, and making soap. Tobacco is the most important cash crop of the village. The villagers also grow vines, figs, and mulberry trees.

However, because the mountain slopes where the villagers grow their crops are steep and stony, the people of Qurdaha are poor and their life is difficult. To get salt to flavor their bread dough, villagers have to make the long trip down to the coast and then carry sacks of sea water back up the mountain. Most families grow wheat and raise goats in order to provide bread, cracked wheat, yogurt, and butter for their diet. Wealthier families might have some vines, fruit trees, and perhaps a flock of sheep.

When the Turks ruled Syria, they neglected the people who lived in the mountains. The result was that their villages did not get the roads, health care, schools, law enforcement, and other social services they needed. The only Turkish government official the mountain people ever saw was the tax collector when he came with soldiers to the village to make the people pay taxes. The real rulers of mountain villages were the heads of powerful, respected families. Sometimes a peasant who earned the respect of the rest of the village could rise to become a village chief.

Asad's grandfather was one such peasant who won a respected place for himself in the village of Qurdaha. His name was Sulayman al-Wahhish (in Arabic *Wahhish* literally means "wild beast"), and it was his great strength, courage, and skill with his fists and gun that earned him the respect of the village. Once when the Turkish governor sent officials to the village to collect taxes and round up recruits for the Turkish army, Sulayman and his friends drove them away with swords and muskets. Qurdaha also respected Asad's grandfather for his fairness as well as for his daring and physical strength. Often the people of the village would come to him to settle feuds and resolve disputes about land boundaries, water rights, and stray animals.

His son, Ali Sulayman, who was born in 1875, was very much like his father. He was also brave, physically strong, skilled with a gun, and respected by the rest of the village. Because people trusted his sense of fairness, they also came to him to settle village quarrels. In the 1920s Ali Sulayman helped the refugees who came south from Aleppo after the French ceded part of the Aleppo district to Turkey. In 1927, after he had become a respected village notable, he changed the family name from Wahhish to Asad, which means "lion" in Arabic.

Ali Sulayman, Asad's father.   **Na'isa, Asad's mother.**

Ali Sulayman had eleven children. He had three sons and two daughters with his first wife. Then, after her death and his remarriage, he had six more children—a daughter and five sons, one of whom was Hafiz. His second wife, Na'isa, who was a strong peasant girl from a village several miles farther up the mountain, was twenty years younger than he was.

The Asad clan lived close together in their part of Qurdaha. The village had no mosque, café, or shop, and the houses, made of mud and rough stone, had no electricity. There was not even a village square or center. So people who wanted to meet and talk had to go to the water spring or the cemetery. Asad's father and uncles owned a few fields. Although they might hire one or two workers to help with the crops, the family did all its own planting, weeding, and harvesting. The family also tended to the vegetable patch and fruit trees and fed the animals.

EARLY LIFE

Hafiz al-Asad was born on October 6, 1930. He was the ninth of Ali Sulayman's eleven children and the fourth of his second marriage. His home was a two-room, flat-roofed stone house. From the front yard a rocky path went downhill to a dirt track that led down the mountain. The family's animals were kept behind the house. Since all of Hafiz's relatives lived close together, he grew up in the warmth of a large, extended family. Although all but two of his ten brothers and sisters were older, his uncle Aziz and his seven younger children lived just down the path. Uncle Aziz's oldest son, Munira, who was a month younger, became Hafiz's closest friend.

Since Hafiz also had three aunts on his father's side who married into families in nearby villages, he had many other cousins to visit. His aunt Sada was to be especially important because the girl whom Hafiz eventually married was a relative of Sada's husband. Hafiz was a young boy when he visited his aunt and met for the first time the girl who would later become his wife. His father's five oldest children by his first marriage were more like uncles and aunts to Hafiz than brothers and sisters. However, their children—Hafiz's nephews and nieces—kept adding fresh faces to his extended family.

His father, who was already 55 when Hafiz was born, was the center of Asad family life. When Hafiz was growing up, his father was already an austere village dignitary who wore a fez and even a tie on certain occasions. His children loved, respected, and obeyed him in all matters. Every morning Hafiz and his brothers kissed their father's hand and would never think of sitting down in his presence. Later the Asad sons who smoked never dared to smoke in front of their father. Hafiz's strong-minded mother, Na'isa, increasingly became the dominant parent for Hafiz and his two younger brothers as their father became more elderly.

Since there was no school in the mountains, Hafiz spent most of his time playing and running about the village with other children or helping with such family chores as watering crops or picking fruit. One of his biggest thrills came when he got to ride the donkey to the family fields.

EDUCATION

Most people in the mountains were illiterate. In fact, it was rare that a village had anyone who could read a letter. It is not surprising, then, that people respected and sought the advice of anybody who knew how to read. A literate person could pass on to the villagers news of the world or entertain them by reading adventure tales from some old book.

Hafiz's father was just such a person. For Qurdaha, which had no electricity and hence no radio, he was its source of news from the outside world, since he subscribed to a newspaper. Although it arrived several days late, the elder Asad kept his village informed of what was happening in the world. During World War II he was the only person in Qurdaha who was able to follow the course of the war and tell the other villagers what was happening. In fact, the map on which he pinpointed the key battles hung in Hafiz's room.

The elder Asad had great respect for book learning. So when the opportunity to give his younger sons an education finally presented itself, he acted. His first eight children had no formal schooling because the Turks had not been interested in educating the people in the mountain villages. Under Turkish rule, village prayer leaders might gather some boys under a tree to teach them their letters and read them passages from the Koran, the Muslim holy book. But Turkish authorities discouraged even this much instruction. If they discovered a prayer leader educating children, they would punish him.

It was the French who began introducing education to remote Alawite villages in the 1930s. When the French allowed a primary school with open-air classes to operate in Qurdaha, the elder Asad secured a place for Hafiz in the new school. Thus Hafiz was the

Latakia is a town situated on the coast of Syria. Asad attended school there.

first of his father's children to receive a formal education. Hafiz became one of the first boys in the village to learn how to read.

In 1939, when Hafiz was nine years old, his father sent him to a school in the coastal town of Latakia for a year. In later life Asad called the experience "the crucial turning point in my life." In Latakia he lived for three months with a married sister. After she moved away with her husband, Hafiz moved into the household of a family acquaintance. For the first time in his life Hafiz mingled with non-Alawites, since most of the people in Latakia were Sunni Muslims or Christians. In Latakia he was introduced to the anti-Alawite prejudice of most Syrians. The Alawites, who numbered only a few hundred, lived in the poorer part of the town where the rest of the people sneered at them.

While Hafiz was in Latakia, World War II broke out in Europe. France was ruling Syria at the time, but after its defeat by Nazi Germany, France was in the hands of a pro-Nazi government. The French in Latakia now feared an attack by the British. They built air-raid shelters, imposed blackouts and censorship, and increased their troop strength in Latakia. Asad later said, "I felt the village was a much safer place and wished I was back home. But I was not much concerned about the Second World War. I was far more worried about my homework."

Hafiz's attention to his homework in Latakia won him good grades and several prizes, which he proudly presented to his father when he returned home in the summer of 1940. Back in his village school, Hafiz continued to do well. He inherited his father's love of learning, and under his guidance he read books and poems and studied the Arabic language. Hafiz's father also encouraged him to develop discipline by learning long poems and then reciting them from memory. The elder Asad would hold contests with his younger sons—Hafiz and his two younger brothers—and then win them himself. Hafiz's excellent memory helped him excel at arithmetic, Arabic, and any other subjects he could learn by heart.

In 1942 Hafiz and three other boys from his village took the examination for the primary school certificate. This certificate would allow them to apply for admission to the secondary school in Latakia. Competition for the school was fierce, since it was the only secondary school in that part of Syria. The principal of the village school had to take the application records for the four boys down to the Latakia secondary school well in advance.

First the four boys rode down the mountain on donkeys to Latakia to have their admissions pictures taken by a photographer. Then they wrote their letters of application, which had to be in their own handwriting and addressed to "His Excellency the Minister of Education" in Latakia. Since the first paragraph of the application letter had to begin a certain distance in from the margin, the boys spent an entire day copying out their application letters, terrified that a single mistake would ruin their chances.

The school principal took the letters, photographs, and birth certificates in a large sealed envelope down to Latakia. Then, when it came time for the admissions examination, the principal advised the boys not to let the examination frighten them. "You are as good as the town boys," he told them. Hafiz and the other three boys from his village passed the examination. Hafiz's score was among the best.

By this time his father was almost 70, so Hafiz began assuming more family responsibilities. He helped his mother with his two younger brothers—Jamil and Rifat. Hafiz was now the member of his family with the most promising future. He was the first of his father's sons to complete a primary education, and now he was about to begin secondary school.

CHAPTER

3

STUDENT
LEADER

I n 1945, when Hafiz returned to Latakia to begin his first year
of secondary school, he was 14. Latakia was a sleepy coastal
town that the Alawites considered their "capital" even though
the town was mostly Sunni Muslim and Christian and Alawites
were treated as outsiders. At the school, Hafiz was one of a handful
of poor mountain boys in the midst of the sons of the wealthy and
powerful landowners, merchants, and religious notables at the top
of Syrian society. Hafiz was shocked at the way these rich boys ran
the school and did whatever they pleased. Years later he recalled:

> They took over the courtyard, beating up boys they didn't
> like and after school they would go to Abu Ali's foodshop

to eat and feed their friends. Poor boys could only look on and go hungry ... Rich boys didn't bother to work, but simply gave themselves what marks they wanted at the end of the year, and very few were the teachers who dared stand up to them.[1]

Poor students like Hafiz had to study extra hard. His love of poetry and his eagerness to learn—the qualities his father had instilled in him—helped place him at the top of his class. Hafiz wrote poetry too. Sometimes after school he would sit by the sea and express his thoughts and feelings in verse. Since Hafiz started school late, he was two years older than most of his classmates. But he was also taller and stronger, and that helped him stand up to the boys who liked to pick on poor mountain boys on the playground. Asad got into many fights defending himself and the other poor boys.

Asad lived in the poor Alawite section of town in a room he shared with a cousin who was his age. There he learned more about the injustices of Syrian society. There were not enough jobs in Latakia to go around for poor people, and local bosses controlled what jobs there were. These bosses sold the jobs to the highest bidders. However, sometimes people were fired before they even got a chance to pay off the local boss. Then the boss sold the job to someone else.

ASAD JOINS THE BAATH PARTY

At the age of 16 Asad took a step that set him on his future course. He joined the Baath party, one of the three main political parties in Syria in the late 1940s. In Arabic the word *ba'th* means "renaissance," or "rebirth." The Baath party called for a rebirth of Arab pride and greatness. The leaders of the Baath party, as well as of the Communist and Syrian Nationalist parties, were fed up with the French. They were also fed up with the Syrian ruling establishment of wealthy city notables and Muslim dignitaries that had allowed foreigners to carve up and rule the country. Since the three parties were determined to shape the course of the new, independent Syria that emerged after World War II, they competed for the minds of young Syrians, especially young men from minority backgrounds like Asad.

While Asad was at the secondary school in Latakia, students like himself in different cities and towns across Syria were arguing about the direction Syria should take. What should the boundaries of modern Syria be? Who should rule the country? How could the power of the old oppressive Syrian ruling class be checked? By joining the Baath party at that time, Asad took part in these important debates about the future of Syria.

The first to use the word *ba'th* as a political term may have been an Alawite intellectual, Zaki al-Arsuzi. A teacher from Antioch who moved to Damascus, Arsuzi taught his young followers that the Arab people would experience a rebirth once they rid themselves of foreign rule. That emancipation would allow Arabs to flourish and take their rightful place in the forefront of civilization.

Two young followers of Arsuzi—a Syrian Christian, Michel Aflaq, and a Syrian Sunni Muslim, Salah al-Din Bitar—set up their own study group in Damascus in 1940. Graduates of the University of Paris like Arsuzi, they became fervent believers in the idea of an Arab rebirth. They wrote and passed out pamphlets; then, in 1942, they gave up their teaching positions to devote themselves full time to advancing their ideas of an Arab *ba'th.*

The main focus of this Baathist movement was on Arab unity. According to Baathist leaders, Arabs would be able to reclaim their proud ancient heritage and advance into a glorious future once they freed themselves from backwardness and foreign domination. "One Arab nation with an eternal message" became the Baathist motto. Aflaq defined the three main principles of the Baathist movement as unity, socialism, and freedom. By "unity" Aflaq meant a single Arab nation united under one government. By "socialism" he meant social justice and economic reform. "Freedom" meant human rights and personal liberty as well as freedom from class conflict and religious strife.

In 1947 the followers of Arsuzi, Aflaq, and Bitar and other supporters of the idea of an Arab rebirth in the Middle East turned the Baathist movement into a political party. Almost 250 young men from Syria and other Arab countries converged on a coffee-house in Damascus. There for three days they shared their dreams of an Arab renaissance, drafted a party constitution, and established an executive committee. The delegates elected Michel Aflaq to head the executive committee of the new Baath party.

The party's emphasis on Arab nationalism and social justice soon attracted many young Alawites, as well as Druzes, Christians, and Sunni Muslims. Many of the early recruits were secondary school students like Asad. But the party also attracted university students and young urban professionals who wanted more rapid economic and social change for Syria than the older, more conservative political leadership was providing. Young Syrians ready to build a strong and just Syrian society free from foreign control found the ideas of the new Baath party attractive.

The Baath party established a base in Latakia through the efforts of a young physician, Dr. Wahib al-Ghanim. While a medical student, he became a follower of Arsuzi. Then, when he began practicing medicine in Latakia in 1943, he spread Arsuzi's ideas of a socialist Arab renaissance. Ghanim attended the founding congress of the Baath party in Damascus and was elected to the party's executive committee. When he returned to Latakia after his election in 1947, he immediately set up a local Baath headquarters at his clinic and began recruiting members.

Asad and his friends were among Ghanim's earliest recruits. At age 16, Asad was already an impressive young man. He was bright, proud, ambitious, physically robust, combative, and unashamed of his Alawite mountain background. After he and his friends joined the party and began working actively for it, Asad's natural abilities

Asad, far right, was a Baath Party student leader in high school.

came to the fore. He quickly emerged as the leader of the local party's younger members.

POLITICAL ACTIVIST

The local Baath party that Asad and his friends worked for was at the forefront of antigovernment demonstrations. These demonstrations often brought Latakia to a standstill. There were running battles with the police as well as fights with rival groups. When the police caught student demonstrators, they beat them and sometimes put them in jail for the night. Besides their participation in these street demonstrations, Asad and his friends collected signatures on petitions, painted party slogans on walls, and copied and distributed Baathist leaflets smuggled in from Damascus.

Although Dr. Ghanim was the source of Baathist ideas in Latakia and the party's link with Damascus, Asad and the other student activists carried the Baathist message to the poor sections of Latakia and to the outlying Alawite villages. Asad wrote his own leaflets and read them to the other students at secret meetings in his room. Then the students copied the leaflets and distributed them. Asad was so skillful at distributing party leaflets that he once succeeded in smuggling them into an army base, much to the amazement of his friends. Asad and his friends also raised money for their poorer classmates whose parents could not afford to pay the school fees.

In 1949, while Asad was still a student, his family moved down the mountain from Qurdaha to Latakia. They lived in a small rooming house while they looked after the youngest member of the family, Rifat, whom they enrolled in school in Latakia. When the elder Asad learned about Hafiz's political activities, he was displeased that his son was not spending more time on his studies.

Under the leadership of Dr. Ghanim and with the help of student activists like Asad, the Baath party made impressive gains in Latakia. Within two years of the party's founding conference, the membership of the party surpassed that of both the Communist party and the Syrian National party. The party's main enemy in Latakia was the Muslim Brotherhood. The Muslim Brothers were fundamentalists who worked to protect and advance the cause of Islam. Started in Syria in the late 1930s, the group was based on the model and teachings of the original Muslim Brotherhood in Egypt. In Latakia the Muslim Brothers were allied to the wealthy conservative Muslim families who ran the town and sent their sons to the school that Asad attended.

As an important Baathist student leader, Asad became a natural target of the local Muslim Brothers. Whenever they saw him, they tried to beat him up. Usually Asad and his friends went out together to protect themselves from these attacks. But once when Asad was alone, a gang of Muslim Brothers caught him and gave him a severe beating. Asad suffered a knife wound in the attack that took several months to heal.

Ghanim did not want the Baath party to appear to be just a party of Alawites and other disgruntled minorities battling against the Sunni Muslim majority. So he urged Alawite party members to keep off the streets and let the Sunni Muslim party members do the street fighting against the Muslim Brothers. But Asad was not one to retreat from a fight. He wanted to be at the center of the battle in the streets for Baathist principles, so Asad refused to stay in the background. He never had sympathized with those Alawites who held themselves back out of fear of asserting themselves and offending the Muslim majority. Eager to find young antiestablishment Sunni Muslims to be his allies in the streets, Asad made many Sunni friends. Many of them remained his friends and allies later in his adult life.

During Asad's last two years at the secondary school, from 1949 to 1951, the students elected him head of the school's student affairs committee. The student affairs committee kept in touch with other school committees across Syria, informing them of student strikes and political rallies. As a result, Asad's reputation and influence spread well beyond Latakia. He made friends with student leaders in other parts of Syria, many of whom later became important figures in Asad's government.

During his last year at the school, Asad gained national attention when the other student leaders of Syria elected him president of the Union of Syrian Students. It was a tremendous honor for Asad, for his family, for the Alawite community, and for the Baath party. By the time Asad graduated in 1951, he had become the most important student leader in Syria. Later Asad spoke about the importance of the years he spent at the Latakia secondary school. "My political life started then," he said, "and has not been interrupted since."

SOURCE—CHAPTER 2
[1]Seale, *Asad*, pp. 24–25

AIR
FORCE

n the summer of 1951 when Asad left Latakia and returned to his home village of Qurdaha, he was 20 years old. Although he had his secondary school diploma and the self-confidence that came with having been a national student leader, he had no clear direction or prospects. His father, uncles, and older brothers were tied to the village life of farming and small-time trade, but Asad had no intention of spending the rest of his life in Qurdaha.

His first ambition had been to become a doctor. In Syria medicine was a prestigious, high-income profession. Being a doctor would have been a big step up the social ladder for a poor mountain boy. In Latakia Asad had been inspired by the example of Dr. Ghanim, who successfully combined medicine and politics. When

Asad received his father's permission to make further inquiries, he telephoned the Jesuit University of Saint Joseph in Beirut, Lebanon, to find out if he could apply to its medical faculty. The university told him there were many papers he would need to fill out, and he would then have to come to the university in person for an interview. Since his father was old and his family had little spare cash to pay for a medical education, Asad never made the trip to Beirut or applied to the medical faculty.

Another possibility for Asad was the Syrian army, which had become an attractive alternative for young men from minority backgrounds. After independence the new Syrian government stopped charging fees at the national military academy at Homs. This made the academy the only institution in the country that poor boys could attend to get ahead in society. Since the academy provided its cadets with food, lodging, and even expense money, it appealed to families who could not afford to send their sons to a university.

After French troops withdrew in 1946, Syria had been left without a national army of its own. When the new government called for volunteers, poor country boys from Alawite and other minority backgrounds signed up in great numbers. They became the backbone of the new Syrian army. After Syria introduced mandatory military service in 1950, boys from well-to-do families served their two years and then returned to their civilian trades and professions. However, since those occupations were closed to poor boys, they stayed on in the army. It was their best chance to get ahead. Asad decided to join the military.

Asad's decision was also influenced by the fact that the Baath party encouraged its young members to enter the military and rise up through its ranks. The army was coming to play an increasingly important role in Syrian political life. Ever since the first military coup in 1949, the barracks of the Syrian office corps had become a hotbed of political debate and intrigue. Since wealthy families steered their sons away from military careers, poor boys from minority backgrounds were able to rise to positions of authority in the army.

MILITARY TRAINING

In the fall of 1951 Asad was one of the ninety young men who enrolled at the military academy at Homs. Asad wanted to be a pilot, but Syria did not yet have an air force academy. However, there was a flying school at Aleppo, which academy cadets could apply to after they passed a physical exam. Asad applied and was chosen to be one of the fifteen cadets admitted to pilot training at the flying school. The flying school was then upgraded to the status of an academy with a special aviation program. The air cadets still received regular army training, but they received extensive air instruction as well.

Asad found there were many advantages to being in the first class at the new air force academy. Since the instructors were new and there were no seniors ahead of Asad's class, the training was pleasantly informal. But the Syrian air force was still undeveloped. Asad and his classmates trained in propeller-driven planes and flew without benefit of radar or ground control. Despite the primitive equipment and easy-going atmosphere, the competition among the 15 air cadets in the academy's first class was fierce. But once again Asad proved himself to be a quick learner. He scored at the top of his class, and at graduation he received an aerobatics trophy.

Asad was a daring flier who liked to display his talent. Since there was no radar and no ground control, once the student pilots were in the air and out of sight nobody knew where they were. Several times Asad flew to Qurdaha to buzz the village and wave to his friends. At the air show his class put on the day before its graduation in 1955, Asad's daring nearly cost him his life. He flew into a dense cloud and avoided a fatal crash only at the very last moment. The day after his close call, he graduated from the academy and became an officer in the Syrian air force.

In 1951 Asad, top, enrolled at the pilot training school at Aleppo.

The air force assigned Asad to the Mezze air base near Damascus. Asad's years as a schoolboy politician in Latakia prepared him well for the intense political debate and infighting that was widespread in the air force officer corps at the time. Although Asad was young and new, he worked hard to win over his fellow officers to the Baathist cause.

At the time the main political division in the officer corps was between the Baath party and the Syrian Social Nationalist party. But soon the Baathists triumphed over their rivals to become the single strongest political force in the armed forces. As a result of the triumph of the Baathists over the Nationalists, the careers of

Asad and the other young Baathist officers advanced. The air force promoted Asad to lieutenant and selected him to go to Cairo, Egypt, for further pilot training. Egypt was the center of Arab rebirth at that time. Cairo was an exciting place for a young Syrian Baathist officer to be.

THE APPEAL OF NASSER'S EGYPT

Egypt's president, Gamal Abdel Nasser, the former army officer who led the overthrow of the king of Egypt in 1952, was fast becoming the star of the Arab world. In 1948 Arab prestige had suffered a severe blow when Arab armies failed to prevent the birth of the new nation, Israel. But now Nasser was increasing Arab pride by challenging Western influence in the Middle East. This was the time of the Cold War—the intense rivalry between the United States and its Western allies and the Soviet Union, China, and their Communist allies. Nasser was daring to alter the delicate Cold War balance of power in the Middle East by threatening to end British and French control of the Suez Canal and by moving Egypt closer to the Soviet Union. The Suez Canal was important to the British and French because it allowed them to trade with Asian countries without having to send their ships around Africa.

During their six-month training course in Cairo, Asad and his fellow Baathist officers became infused with Nasser's spirit of Arab nationalism and the prospect of an Arab rebirth led by Nasser's Egypt. Asad also got to fly Egypt's modern British-built jets instead of the old propeller-driven planes he was used to back in Syria. By the time Asad and his fellow Baathist officers were ready to return from Egypt in early 1956, they realized that Nasser's ideas were so close to Syrian Baathist ideas that they talked about the desirability of a union of the two countries.

In the summer of 1956 Syrian Baathist enthusiasm for Nasser increased even more when Nasser defied the British and French by announcing he was nationalizing the Suez Canal. His bold action of taking control of the canal away from the two former colonial masters of the Middle East was highly popular throughout the Arab world. Syria was so enthusiastic that it offered to assist Egypt militarily, but it was too late. Britain, France, and Israel took steps against Egypt to recover the Suez Canal. Israeli forces advanced with lightning speed into the Sinai Peninsula. However, the United Nations quickly stepped into the conflict. It ordered the withdrawal of the attacking Israeli forces and then sent UN troops to keep peace on the border between Egypt and Israel.

During this Suez crisis the Syrian air force sent Asad north to an air base near Aleppo to fly fact-finding missions over northern and eastern Syria. Late one afternoon he received an order to go up and intercept an unidentified aircraft. He had tested his brakes before takeoff and had found them faulty, but he decided to risk it anyway. He took off and circled far and wide over northeastern Syria, but he didn't find the aircraft he was sent up to intercept. When Asad returned to his base, it was night. Not only was his plane not equipped for night flying, but when Asad tried to radio the airport to find out the wind direction, he discovered his radio was dead.

Asad tried to land in the darkness. He overshot the runway because of a strong tail wind and his faulty brakes. As his plane raced across a field toward a stone wall, the wheels hit a water pipe and vaulted up over the wall. The wheels flew off, but the plane miraculously landed on its belly. Asad jumped quickly out of the plane and dove into a ditch, certain that the smoking plane was going to explode. Asad was lucky to be alive. When the rescuers arrived, they were amazed he was still in one piece. Once more Asad narrowly escaped death.

In early 1958 the Syrian Baathist dream came true. Egypt and Syria joined each other in a political union called the United Arab Republic (UAR). Syrian Baathists were overjoyed, since they regarded Nasser as the greatest living Arab leader and the one most likely to unite the rest of the Arabs. The United Arab Republic united Egypt and Syria under a single president—Nasser—and

In 1958 President Nasser of Egypt, center, joined Egypt and Syria into a political union called the United Arab Republic.

merged their armed forces. Asad and his young fellow officers were optimistic. They had great faith in Nasser's leadership, his commitment to Arab unity, and his willingness to stand up to the Western powers.

MARRIAGE

In the same year of the union of Egypt and Syria—1958—Asad decided to marry Aniseh Makhlaf. Aniseh was a young woman from the village of Bustan al-Basha whom he had known since childhood. His aunt Sada had married into the Makhlaf family, so Asad had visited the village often while he was growing up. However, after he returned from his training course in Egypt, he looked at Aniseh with new eyes. Educated at a French convent school at Banyas on the coast, she was now a young schoolteacher—slim, dark-haired, and well-mannered. They fell in love, and when Asad asked her to marry him, she agreed.

At first Aniseh's father was against the marriage. Since he was loyal to the Syrian Nationalist party, he was not happy about the prospect of having a zealous Baathist air force lieutenant for a son-in-law. Also, Aniseh's family was from a higher social class. Asad's ancestors were peasants, but Aniseh's had been notables in their village for many generations. However, his aunt Sada and Aniseh's mother were impressed by Asad, and Aniseh herself liked his integrity and intelligence. So Asad persisted until he finally won Aniseh's father over. After he gave the young couple his permission, they went to Damascus where a religious notary married them.

Asad and Aniseh spent the first years of their marriage in very modest housing near the air base in a poor district of Mezze. Aniseh had to live in poorer circumstances than she was used to, but she did not complain. She loved her husband and became a devoted wife and mother. Through the years she provided Asad with a foundation of domestic stability and family security.

After they were married for only a few weeks, they had to be separated. Asad was one of a select number of Syrian pilots whom the air force had chosen to send to the Soviet Union. The training course was to teach Syria's best pilots how to fly Soviet MIG fighters at night. In this era of rivalry between the Cold War superpowers—the United States and the Soviet Union—for influence in the Middle East, both Syria and Egypt were moving closer to the Soviet Union. Like Egypt, Syria was also becoming increasingly dependent on the USSR for weapons supplies, especially modern Soviet MIG fighter planes. The assignment, which was a plus for

Asad's air force career, was an untimely interruption of the young marriage. Aniseh was pregnant with their first child when she and Asad's family and friends saw him off.

During Asad's ten months in the Soviet Union, Aniseh stayed with her family in her home village. Also during this time she gave birth to their daughter, Bushra. When Asad returned from the USSR in the spring of 1959, he rushed home to the mountains to see his wife and new baby. Asad then visited Qurdaha, where he was received like a national hero. Everybody came to see him, and the feasting, singing, and dancing went on well into the night. When Asad reported back to the air force headquarters in Damascus, he was disappointed to learn that the union of Egypt and Syria was already beginning to turn sour.

THE UNITED ARAB REPUBLIC CRUMBLES

Syrian Baathists had at first been enthusiastic about Syria's union with Egypt. After all, Nasser was a champion of Baathist ideas. Also, his position as head of the United Arab Republic strengthened him as the main spokesperson for the Arab cause throughout the world. Syrian Baathists were also happy that the union was helping to check the interests of their pro-Communist and conservative rivals inside Syria.

However, it soon dawned on Syrian Baathists that the union was weakening their own interests as well. Egypt and Syria were supposed to be equal partners in the United Arab Republic, with Syria as the northern district and Egypt as the southern district. However, as the stronger partner, Egypt soon began to dominate the union. Nasser imposed higher taxes on Syrians, issued import restrictions, and dissolved all Syrian political parties, including the Baath party.

Nasser also dominated the Syrian military. The Egyptian and pro-Nasser Syrian officers he put in charge of the Syrian armed forces proceeded to crack down on dissenters. During the three years of the existence of the UAR (1958–1961), Egyptian and Syrian Nasserites purged 11,000 officers from the Syrian armed forces. However, this widespread purge of senior military officers did help junior officers like Asad. He was promoted to captain, moving up more quickly than he would have ordinarily.

In 1959 Asad returned to Cairo as a result of the Egyptian reorganization of the Syrian armed forces. The Egyptians transferred the Aleppo air force academy and part of the Homs military academy to Egypt. Egypt also shifted Asad's squadron of night-flying MIG-19 jet fighters to Cairo.

In Cairo Asad and other Syrian officers spent their free time in cafés discussing politics. By early 1960 Asad was meeting secretly with four other young Baathist officers who found they shared the same hopes and concerns for Syria's future. This group of five officers—all from minority backgrounds (three Alawites and two Ismailis)—called itself the Military Committee. They shared a growing dissatisfaction with Egyptian control of the Syrian government and military and with the civilian leaders of the Syrian Baath party who had let the Egyptians dissolve their party. They feared that the wealthy landowners and merchants who once ran Syria were getting stronger.

Asad and the other young officers of the Military Committee saw themselves as true guardians of Baathist principles and Syrian progress. They vowed to rebuild the shattered Baath party and fight against the reemergence of the old political order. They also wanted to protect the right of Alawites, Ismailis, and other minorities to advance in the military and in Syrian society. Since the Military Committee members knew the Egyptians did not trust them, they met secretly in their apartments to discuss strategy or took day trips out of Cairo.

Syrian dissatisfaction with the United Arab Republic finally came to a head on September 28, 1961 when the Syrian army revolted against Egyptian rule. The army established a new civilian government in Damascus that immediately declared Syria's secession from the UAR. Nasser was shocked and outraged. At first he wanted to send in paratroopers to crush the Syrian revolt, but he thought better of it.

The stay of Asad and his wife in Egypt at this time proved an eventful one. Shortly after they arrived in Cairo, their infant daughter Bushra had become ill and died. A fellow officer remembered how deeply Asad felt the loss of his only child as he knelt by his dying daughter's bedside and cried. However, in October 1960, while they were still in Cairo, Aniseh gave birth to another daughter whom they named Bushra after their deceased firstborn.

Asad and his colleagues who were still in Egypt when Syria pulled out of the UAR were trapped. Asad managed to have a friend escort his wife and baby daughter back to Syria by sea, but the Egyptians put Asad in prison. He stayed there for a month and a half before he and the other imprisoned Syrian officers were released. They were part of a prison exchange the two countries worked out. Asad and the other Syrians were returned in exchange for Egyptian officers held in Syria.

When Asad arrived back in Damascus, he was horrified to learn that the new Syrian government was purging Baathist officers who had supported the union from the armed forces. The government promptly expelled Asad and the other four members of the Military Committee, together with fifty-eight other Baathist officers from the armed forces. The purged officers were given low-level jobs in various government ministries. Asad found himself consigned to an insignificant desk job in the Department of Maritime Transport in the Ministry of Economics.

However, Asad did not give up. He and the other four members of the Military Committee, all now working in obscure civilian jobs in the government bureaucracy, continued to meet secretly. They decided to broaden the committee and make contact with others willing to oppose the new government.

In March 1962 a failed coup attempt against the government forced Asad to flee across the border into Lebanon. However, Asad was caught by Lebanese authorities and put in jail. They questioned him closely for a week before they sent him back to Syria where the government's suspicion of Asad made him a marked man. One week after Aniseh gave birth to their first son, Basil, the police raided Asad's home to look for evidence that he was plotting against the government.

This was a terrible time for Asad. Suddenly it looked as if his luck had run out. For a long time he had known only success as student leader, daring pilot (narrowly escaping death twice), home-town hero, new husband and father, and popular air force officer. But now all that had changed. Now sacked from the air force, Asad was a lowly government clerk without money or prospects, and the government had him pegged as a troublemaker. Asad's promising career seemed over.

CHAPTER
5

RISE
TO
POWER

Asad and his allies on the Military Committee spent the remaining months of 1962 secretly plotting against the government. Since they were young (Asad was only 31), inexperienced, and outside the armed forces, they looked for allies inside the officer corps, where dissatisfaction with the government was widespread. Because the government consisted of the privileged groups of the former power structure, it was weak and unpopular. So it had plenty of enemies, especially inside the officer corps.

The Military Committee recruited Baathists and officers loyal to Nasser who resented the government's decision to secede from Egypt. After several high-ranking Nasserite officers agreed to join the plot, the conspirators formed a six-man group to direct the coup. This group consisted of the three original members of the Military Committee (Umran, Jadid, and Asad), two Nasserite officers, and a prominent commander whom they persuaded to join the antigovernment plot.

In the meantime, Asad and his fellow Baathist officers mended their fences with Aflaq and the other civilian leaders of the Baath party. In the spring of 1962 the first party congress in Syria since Egypt dissolved the party in 1958 reestablished Aflaq as leader of the revived Baath party. When the Military Committee informed Aflaq of its plan to seize control of the government, he gave his support.

BAATHISTS SEIZE POWER—1963

In Iraq there was a successful Baathist coup in February 1963. This Baathist success in Syria's Arab neighbor to the east inspired Syrian Baathists and gave them confidence that they too could seize power. By early March 1963 the six-man group of conspirators decided they had lined up enough military support to move against the government. On the night of March 7, armed troops and tank units under the control of Baathist officers moved swiftly into Damascus. They seized control of key positions—army communications, the central post office, the radio station, and the Ministry of Defense.

Asad led the force that seized the Dumayr air base outside of Damascus, where most of the Syrian air force was located. The well-organized coup struck with such lightning speed that the stunned government fell without the shedding of any blood. Suddenly the Military Committee found itself transformed into the most powerful political force in the country.

The first act of the victorious conspirators was to reinstate in the armed forces the members of the Military Committee and all the other Baathist officers whom the military had expelled. Asad became the new commander of the Dumayr air base. He was then rapidly promoted from captain to major to lieutenant-colonel. By the end of 1963 Asad was virtually in charge of the entire Syrian air force.

Needing somebody to head the government whom it could control from behind the scenes, the Military Committee selected Colonel Amin al-Hafiz. Hafiz was not a Baathist, but he was a respected Sunni Muslim officer whom Asad and his allies had known in Egypt. In a country with a Sunni Muslim majority, the choice of Hafiz was a good one. The members of the Military Committee persuaded him to serve in the critical position of minister of the interior.

NEW DIVISIONS

The main threat to the new Baathist government came from Nasser's supporters who wanted to bring Syria back into union with Nasser's Egypt. The Military Committee moved swiftly to contain the threat by purging the armed forces of pro-Nasser officers and replacing them with Baathists. When the Nasserites attacked the Damascus radio station and army headquarters in order to seize control of the government, the Baathists crushed the revolt, killing hundreds of Nasser supporters. When Nasser denounced the Syrian Baathists as murderers, the break between Egypt and Syria was complete.

The Military Committee succeeded in eliminating all organized resistance to their rule within four months of their coup. However, inside the Baath party a struggle was in progress about how the Baath party was to rule Syria and who was going to be in charge of the government. Was it going to be the civilian veterans of the Baath party, headed by its founder, Michel Aflaq? Or was it going to be the young Baathist officers, headed by the Military Committee?

After Asad was elected to the new eight-man Regional Command of the party, he took part in these debates about programs the party should advocate. In the fall of 1963 at both the regional and national party congresses, Asad and his fellow officers advocated radical solutions to Syrian problems. They wanted programs to help the peasants, workers, and minority members whom the rich and privileged of Syria had ignored for so long. Making their voices heard at the party congresses, Asad and his fellow officers succeeded in getting military Baathists (Jadid and Hafiz) elected as members of the party's National Command for the first time.

In 1964 Asad was made commander of the Syrian air force. He was also promoted to major-general. Asad's standing in the Baath party, the government, and the Military Committee increased greatly. The party gave Asad the important responsibility of organizing the Syrian armed forces along Baath party lines. Working day and night, he built a hierarchical structure of divisions, sections, and branches throughout the military. His impressive organizational achievement strengthened his command over the armed forces. This control over the military was to prove his greatest asset in the power struggles ahead.

A junior partner behind Umran and Jadid in the Military Committee, Asad was content to work behind the scenes while the older men—Umran, Jadid, and the nominal head of state, Hafiz—shared the spotlight. As Asad worked quietly to advance the Baathist principles he believed in, he was patiently building his military power base.

Further divisions inside the party and government developed when the two leading members of the Military Committee—Umran and Jadid—split over government matters. Umran advocated more moderate measures, Jadid more radical ones. The division between the two men was the first open breach in the Military Committee. At first Asad tried to heal the split between his two older allies. However, when he found out he could not prevent the growing rift, Asad supported Jadid.

Umran sought the support of Aflaq and the other civilian Baathist leaders. But Jadid and Asad were able to strip him of his posts in the party and government and send him off to be Syria's ambassador to Spain. With Umran gone, Asad gained even more control over the military. Umran had headed the small defense force the Military Committee had set up to protect itself against possible attacks. Now that this defense force needed a new commander, Asad put his younger brother, Rifat, in charge. Seven years younger than Asad, Rifat had followed his brother into the military and was now benefiting from Asad's rise to power.

The growing split between Aflaq and the civilian Baathists on the one hand and Jadid, Asad, and the radical officers on the other created yet another crisis inside the Syrian government. At the national congress of the Baath party in 1965, Aflaq tried to regain control of the party, which had been slipping more and more into the hands of the officers. Hafiz, who had become disillusioned with his role in the government as the front man for Jadid and Asad, suddenly changed sides. He withdrew his support from Jadid and Asad and gave it to Aflaq and the other civilian Baathist leaders.

In December 1965 the old-guard Baathist civilians made their move against Jadid, Asad, and the radical officers. They got the Baath party congress to declare a new government, with Hafiz and the exiled Umran as its leaders. Although Asad sided with his longtime ally, Jadid, he felt disheartened about this split in the Baath party. As tensions increased, Asad went away to London for medical treatment. His back and neck, which he injured in the crash landing he made during his pilot training, needed medical attention. Asad was only too happy to get away from the party feud. However, when he returned to Syria, he found the conflict approaching a showdown.

THE 1966 COUP

The crisis reached its violent climax in February 1966. When Hafiz ordered the transfer of three of Jadid's supporters from their

The 1966 coup that brought radical Baathists to power in Syria resulted in a promotion for Asad. He became minister of defense in the new government.

military commands, Jadid's forces attacked Hafiz at his home. After a raging battle between the two sides, Hafiz surrendered. The Military Committee put Hafiz, Umran, and commanders loyal to them in prison. Jadid's side then purged more than 400 of their opponents from the army, party, and government. Jadid also rounded up Bitar and other veteran Baathists. Aflaq was able to escape to Lebanon.

Whatever qualms Asad may have had about using such force to end the party feud, he ended up playing a leading role in the showdown. Even though his air force was not needed, Asad called officers across the country to urge them to support Jadid and the

Military Committee and not Hafiz, Umran, and the Baathist civilians. With the Jadid forces victorious, once more Asad was on the winning side. Jadid rewarded Asad for his crucial support by making him the new minister of defense. Asad was now a member of the cabinet. At the age of only 35, he was at the very center of power in the new government.

Asad played a leading role in helping the new regime consolidate its power and advance its radical Baathist program. Although the new Jadid government was young and inexperienced, it was determined to implement the Baathist principles of rooting out privilege and corruption and improving the lot of peasants, workers, and minorities. The new regime set about purging the rich and powerful from the government. The new Jadid government also took over management of private and religious schools, which had been in the hands of wealthy Sunni Muslims. While Jadid ran the government and implemented his radical program, Asad concentrated on keeping the armed forces loyal to the new government—and to himself.

THE 1967 WAR WITH ISRAEL

As defense minister, Asad faced his greatest challenge against Syria's bitter enemy, Israel. Syria had lost a war with Israel in 1948–1949 and had engaged in a long-running border conflict with Israel over disputed land on the eastern shore of the Sea of Galilee. After Asad became defense minister, he stepped up these border battles. Asad also assisted Palestinian guerrilla raids from Syrian territory into Israel.

Tensions increased. Israel felt increasingly threatened by the circle of belligerent Arab countries that surrounded it. Syria and Egypt signed a military pact in November 1966. Then, in May 1967, Egypt and Jordan signed a pact as well. On June 5, 1967, these Israeli-Arab tensions finally exploded. Early in the morning Israel launched a surprise attack against its Arab enemies. The Israeli air force smashed the Arab air forces while their planes were

In 1967 Israel launched a surprise attack on its Arab enemies. In a six-day war, Israel completely defeated Syria and humiliated Asad. Here, Israeli boats patrol the Strait of Tiran.

still on the ground. Without air support, the Arab armies were no match for the Israelis. Israel's armies were victorious on all fronts. The Israelis routed the Egyptians in the Sinai and the Jordanians on the west bank of the Jordan River. On the Syrian front the Israelis stormed the Golan Heights and captured the city of Quneitra.

By the time a cease-fire went into effect on June 10, the Israelis were pushing the Syrians back toward Damascus. The war, brief but decisive, was a nightmare for Asad. As defense minister of Syria, he lost both the Syrian air force and the Golan Heights.

ASAD SEIZES POWER

In the aftermath of this humiliating defeat, Syrians blamed each other. The civilian members of the government blamed Asad and the military for losing the war, while the armed forces blamed the civilians for letting Syria get dragged into the war without an adequate national defense. Resentment and distrust widened the gap between the armed forces under Asad and the government under Jadid.

Asad tried to pressure the government into spending more on the armed forces. In early 1968 he tightened his control over the military by making his longtime friend, Mustafa Tlas, chief of staff in place of a Jadid supporter. Asad also purged Jadid loyalists and replaced them with his own supporters in other key areas of the military. Asad integrated the paramilitary organizations of the Baath party into the army as well. As Asad's attempt to increase his influence in the government and the party met firm resistance from Jadid and his supporters, the Syrian regime became hopelessly divided. Jadid and Asad supporters refused to speak to each other.

In the fall of 1970, these tensions came to a boil. Jadid called an emergency meeting of the national congress of the Baath party to strip Asad and Tlas of their positions. But Asad was ready to meet the challenge. On November 16, 1970, while the emergency meeting was still in session, Asad ordered his soldiers to surround the conference hall. Then, when the meeting broke up, Asad arrested Jadid and his supporters and sent them to prison. He put Jadid in the Mezze prison in Damascus, where he remains to this day.

Now Hafiz al-Asad, the son of a poor Alawite mountain family, was Syria's new strongman. Since most Syrians had grown to dislike Jadid's government, they hoped the change of rulers would be a good one for the country.

PRESIDENT

fter Asad seized control of the government, he moved quickly to broaden his base of support. With the Syrian people ready for a more conciliatory regime after years of division and conflict, Asad presented himself as a popular, national leader and his regime as constitutional and democratic. He wanted to give the impression that his authority came from the people, not just from the army or the Baath party. Speaking of his coup against Jadid as a "corrective movement made in response to our people's demands and aspirations," he set out on a course of national reconciliation.

Asad spent his first days in power receiving delegations that came to Damascus from all over the country to offer their congratulations. Unlike previous rulers, Asad went out into the countryside to meet people and listen to their problems. Crowds greeted him everywhere he went. After every visit outside Damascus, he returned with bags of petitions and complaints, which he had his staff sort out and take care of.

At first Asad held back from assuming the highest position in the government, preferring instead to rule Syria from behind the scenes in the manner of his predecessors. After his coup, he put forward a young, little-known Sunni Muslim teacher to be head of state, since by tradition the head of the country always belonged to the Sunni Muslim majority. Asad took the less prestigious title of prime minister while holding all the real power. However, this arrangement did not agree with Asad for long. Ever since his days as a student politician, he had been used to thrusting himself forward. Staying in the background was not natural for him. So, on February 22, 1971, Asad resigned from the air force and assumed "presidential powers."

Wanting the support of the people, Asad called for a vote to approve his seven-year presidential term. The referendum, which was held on March 12, 1971, endorsed him for the presidency with a vote of 99.2 percent. Since then, Asad has held similar presidential referenda every seven years to allow the people the chance to endorse his presidential terms. In 1978, 99.6 percent of the voters approved his new term, while in 1985 the vote was 99.9 percent. The next vote is scheduled for 1992. These referenda were not real elections, since there were no other candidates to vote for. Nevertheless, Asad used the overwhelming vote totals to strengthen his rule. Each presidential referendum allows him to claim that his regime is democratic and that he has the support of the people.

A NEW CONSTITUTION

Asad wanted his new government to have a new constitution. Shortly after he took power, he had the Provisional Regional Com-

President Asad and Syrian leaders at prayer. Asad has gone to great lengths to show himself as a devout Muslim.

mand of the Baath party nominate candidates for an assembly. The purpose of the assembly, called the People's Assembly, was to draft a constitution. A national referendum was called to approve the 173 candidates, who were drawn from a wide range of Syrian social groups. In 1972 this same People's Assembly became the country's new parliament.

The constitution that the People's Assembly drafted made President Asad the sole ruler of Syria by declaring him both head of the government and commander of the armed forces. It gave him power to appoint all the vice-presidents, cabinet ministers, and other important officials of the government. The constitution also gave Asad the final authority over the Supreme Council of Magistrates and the People's Assembly. Asad received the power to refer any matter to a national referendum and to mobilize the army and declare war. The new constitution made Syria one of the most centralized governments in the Middle East, giving Asad more power than most rulers.

After the constitution was published on January 31, 1973, it was presented to the people for their approval. Many Sunni Muslims objected that the new constitution had no article stating that the head of the Syrian state had to be a Muslim. All the constitutions of earlier Syrian governments had provided such an article. Asad responded to the Muslim objection by allowing a religion article to be added to the constitution.

However, he made sure nobody tried to use the clause against him by claiming that he was not a true Muslim just because he was an Alawite. Most Sunni Muslims looked down on Alawites and regarded them as heretics rather than authentic Muslims. To settle the matter, Asad appealed to the influential religious leader Imam Musa al-Sadr for a ruling. The Imam was head of all Shiite Muslims in Lebanon and Syria. When the Imam declared that Alawites were an authentic Shiite Muslim community, he defused the issue and removed a potential thorn from the side of the Asad presidency.

However, when Syrian Muslims went so far as to insist that the new constitution make Islam Syria's official religion, Asad fought against their move. Having personally known the discrimination the Sunni Muslim majority directed against Alawites and other minorities, Asad fiercely opposed all attempts by Sunni Muslims to impose their way of life on the country's non-Sunni minorities. When Asad finally presented the new constitution to the Syrian people for their approval in a referendum on March 12, 1973, they gave it their overwhelming endorsement.

THE BAATH PARTY

Asad was a fervent believer in the principles of the Baath party. Ever since his student days in Latakia and his early days in the air force, he had worked tirelessly to promote the interests and ideals of the party. Later, as defense minister, he organized the entire armed forces along Baath party lines. Now that he was Syria's sole ruler, Asad moved to strengthen the party and make it a more effective instrument of his will.

As secretary-general of the Baath party, Asad appointed his supporters to a 14-member Provisional Regional Command, which he later expanded to 21 members. The group's purpose was to discuss government policy and make recommendations. Although Asad made all the final decisions, this group of advisers met regularly throughout Asad's presidency to help him govern.

Previously the Baath party had been little more than a debating society. However, after the Baathists came to power, the party began to function as an instrument of government. After Asad came to power, he made it even more of a ruling party. Beginning in April 1971, Baath party members throughout Syria elected delegates to regional and national congresses. At these party congresses, now held every four years or so, several hundred party delegates from all over Syria meet in an atmosphere of "party democracy" to elect party leaders and lay down party guidelines. Asad often makes his most important speeches and policy statements before these congresses.

Not only did Asad give new life to the party congresses but he strengthened the party-controlled organizations. These organizations helped mobilize support for Asad's regime among peasants, workers, students, women, young people, and other special groups within Syrian society. Many of these groups, long excluded from power and influence in Syrian society, now felt they had a champion in Asad and a voice in his new Baathist government.

Asad tightened his grip on the party further by purging it of his opponents. Although Aflaq and Hafiz had taken refuge in Iraq, their supporters remained in the party. In 1971 Asad had the party put Aflaq and Hafiz on trial *in absentia* for treason. Death sentences were handed down on Aflaq, Hafiz, and three of their supporters who had fled the country. About 100 of their supporters in Syria were sent to prison. Although Asad later took back the death sentences and released most of those who had been imprisoned, the trial served as a warning that he would tolerate no disloyalty.

One of Asad's enemies who remained a threat was one of the original leaders of the Military Committee, Muhammad Umran. Umran had escaped to Lebanon after he was ousted from power in the 1966 coup. Now from his home in the Lebanese coastal city of Tripoli, he plotted against Asad in hopes of returning to Syria and recapturing control of the government.

However, Umran made a fatal mistake: he wrote Asad and informed him of his plans. One week before Umran was to return to Syria, two assassins murdered him in his home. Although they were never brought to justice, many suspected Asad was behind it. They assumed either he ordered the killing himself or his security forces arranged it on his behalf. The assassins were said to be Palestinians, but the mystery of who was responsible for the murder remained. With Umran's assassination, a dangerous threat to Asad's rule was suddenly removed. With Jadid in prison, Asad was now the only original member of the Military Committee left.

In March 1972 Asad sought to broaden the support for his regime beyond the Baath party by establishing the National Progressive Front. The front consisted of four other political parties whose goals were similar to those of the Baathists. These were the Communist party, the Arab Socialist Union, the Socialist Unionists, and the Arab Socialist party. Since these parties also wanted a radical transformation of Syrian society, their support was useful. Asad gave several of their leaders important positions in the government. However, he did not allow these parties to seek new members in the armed forces or schools.

LOCAL GOVERNMENT

Asad established a system of local government that allowed Syrians to practice a form of "popular democracy." On March 3, 1972, Syrians went to the ballot box to elect local councils in each of the country's fourteen political districts. At least half of the candidates for these councils had to be peasants or workers. The rest could come from any other walk of life.

Many candidates were Baathists or members of the National Progressive Front, but there were independents as well. In fact, independents won a majority of places on the councils in both Damascus and Homs. Asad described these elections as "the first elections in this country that were marked by freedom and fairness." They showed that early in his rule Asad was willing to tolerate some democracy and diversity of opinion, at least on the local level.

In each district these local councils helped the governor run his district. Although the councils met only every three months, their executive boards usually met with the governor every day. In Damascus and Aleppo the councils had 100 members, 10 of whom served on the executive board. At the local level these popularly elected councils had the power to initiate projects and raise the taxes to finance them.

In the first years of his rule in the early 1970s, Asad summoned the Syrian people to the ballot box five times. They voted to confirm him as president, to elect representatives to the People's Assembly, to approve the new constitution, to elect local councils, and finally, in September 1972, to vote on Syria's proposed federation with Egypt and Libya. The union of the three countries—to be called the Federation of Arab Republics—never materialized.

These referenda and the campaigns Asad's government launched to explain the issues to the public and enlist their support made Syrians feel they were included in the important decisions of their government. Although these national votes made Syria seem more a "people's democracy" than it was in reality, they were a marked improvement over the practice of earlier Syrian regimes, which did little to seek popular support.

GOVERNMENT AND THE SECRET INNER SECURITY CORE

From the beginning Asad's regime has consisted of two parts—public and private. The public part is the government itself, which is the formal structure of political and economic affairs that keeps the country running on a day-to-day basis. The private part of Asad's regime is the hidden inner core of his security forces—the army, police, and security services. This is the security core Asad relies on to protect himself and his government.

The public part is the outer layer of government and public affairs that Syrians see. This is the part that is diverse, open to talent, and mainly Sunni Muslim. The Sunnis, who are a 70 percent majority of the Syrian population, continue to hold most of the senior positions in the cabinet, party, and government. In fact, all of Syria's prime ministers, defense ministers, and foreign ministers have been Sunni Muslims. Mustafa Tlas, Asad's friend since his days as a student politician, is defense minister and deputy commander of the army. Another Sunni, Abd al-Halim Khaddam, is foreign minister, deputy prime minister, and vice-president.

However, the private part of the regime—the secret inner security core that Asad depends on to protect his life and maintain his power—is solidly Alawite. Asad is the first Alawite ever to rule Syria openly, unlike his predecessor, Jadid, who ruled Syria from behind the scenes. The powerful heads of the secret police units and chiefs of the special military forces who protect Asad and his regime are invisible to the public. Since their names and pictures never appear in the press, most Syrians do not know who these men are. Yet apart from Asad himself, the chiefs of his inner security core are the only other people in Syria with real power.

Asad uses both the outer layer of government and the inner layer of security, whether Sunni Muslim or Alawite, to rule Syria and maintain his power. All aspects of government, party, and army and security forces are utilized to extend Asad's control at every level of Syrian society. Asad made many enemies on his way to the top, and his enemies would only be too happy to bring down his Alawite-dominated regime and end his life. That is why Asad needs a tight security apparatus that reaches into every corner of Syrian life.

In each provincial district there are three important men—the governor, the party secretary, and the head of political security— and they all check on each other. The governor and the party secretary keep an eye on each other, while the security chief keeps an eye on both of them. For all three men the chain of command extends to Damascus and all the way up to Asad himself. This complex network has allowed Asad to control Syria and remain in power for more than twenty years.

CHAPTER

THE STRUGGLE AGAINST ISRAEL

A sad never got over the humiliating defeat Israel inflicted
on Syria in 1967 when he was defense minister. So from
the moment he came to power in 1970, he embarked on a
crusade to wage war against Israel again. He wanted to win back
the Golan Heights, that part of southern Syria that bordered northern Israel which the Israelis now occupied. Asad thought of himself
as a latter-day Saladin, the Islamic warrior-hero of the Middle Ages
who defeated the European Crusaders and helped drive them out of
the Middle East. As a modern Saladin, Asad wanted to transform
the balance of power in the Middle East by defeating the Israelis
and driving them into the sea.

In 1971 Asad allocated over 70 percent of the Syrian budget to the armed forces. Money that might have been spent on schools, roads, and power plants went into the military buildup. Asad made many speeches to the Syrian people to prepare them psychologically for a war against Israel. He wanted them to win back their land and to convince them of the need to make sacrifices.

The Arabs and Israelis were now locked in a dangerous state of armed confrontation. With the Cold War superpowers—the United States and the Soviet Union—on opposite sides of the conflict, the Middle East was a powder keg ready to explode. While the United States supported and armed Israel, the Soviet Union supported and armed Syria and Egypt.

Asad needed Soviet weapons for his military buildup. So, in July 1972, he went to Moscow to sign an arms deal. He spent $700 million to purchase MIG-21s, SAM-6 antiaircraft missiles, FROG surface-to-surface missiles, and other advanced weapons that he needed against Israel. Israel, in turn, fortified itself with the weapons it needed from the United States and other Western nations. The Middle East was in a dangerous arms race as both superpowers supplied its Middle Eastern allies with advanced military hardware.

The Soviet Union sent military advisers as well as weapons to Syria. In 1972 the number of Soviet advisers in Syria jumped from 700 to 3,000. In February 1973 the visit of a Soviet military delegation to Damascus led to another large delivery of tanks and other weapons. In early May, Asad visited Moscow again and returned with a high-level military delegation, headed by the chief of the Soviet air force. The Soviets then delivered more SAM-6 antiaircraft missiles.

By this time the Soviets began to worry that Syria wanted their weapons in order to start a war with Israel. Since the Soviet Union wanted a political settlement of the Arab-Israeli conflict, its policy was to deliver weapons primarily defensive in nature. The Soviets wanted to help Syria protect itself against an Israeli attack as well as strengthen Syria's negotiating hand. The Soviets did not want

President Asad greets Egyptian leader Anwar Sadat. In 1973 both leaders agreed to launch an attack on their common enemy, Israel.

Syria to start another war against Israel. They feared another Syrian defeat would be a heavy blow to Soviet interests and prestige in the region. When Syria requested the latest Soviet MIG-23 jet fighters, the Soviet Union refused.

However, no amount of Soviet caution could have turned Asad aside from his determination to wage war. He was realistic enough to know he would need help on the battlefield, since Israel's army was stronger than Syria's. For that reason, Asad signed a military pact with Egypt barely two weeks after he seized power in 1970. Asad needed the help of other Arabs—certainly Egypt and perhaps Jordan and Iraq as well.

Asad concluded that war was the only way he was ever going to get the Golan Heights back, since Israel seemed in no mood to accept a peaceful solution to the problem. In December 1972 Asad told an Indian journalist that he thought a war with Israel was inevitable if a political settlement could not be worked out in the next few months. The Israelis enraged Asad further in late 1972 and early 1973 by attacking Syrian positions and inflicting heavy casualties. Since Syria was allied with the Palestine Liberation Organization (PLO), Israel wanted to punish Syria for sponsoring PLO attacks against Israel.

ASAD PREPARES FOR WAR

When the new Egyptian war minister came to Damascus in February 1973 with a plan for an Egyptian-Syrian offensive against Israel, Asad quickly agreed. Egypt's President Sadat wanted to attack in May, but that was too soon for Asad. He needed more time to prepare. So Sadat agreed to move the invasion date to October. Having made the decision to go to war, Asad paid a secret visit to Cairo to coordinate plans for the joint operation. Asad also went to Moscow to try to patch up Egyptian-Soviet relations. Sadat had expelled the Soviets from Egypt in 1972, so Asad wanted to restore relations between his two allies in hopes of resuming the flow of Soviet weapons to Egypt before the invasion.

Asad and Sadat worked to improve their relations with King Hussein of Jordan in hopes of drawing him into their war plans Asad was especially interested in winning the king over. Since Jordan had a long border with Israel, Syria would be in a stronger position if it could attack Israel through Jordan as well as on the Golan Heights. However, King Hussein refused to commit himself to the Egyptian-Syrian operation. But he did dispatch two brigades to the Golan Heights as a gesture of Arab solidarity.

Asad also had to worry about an Israeli attack through Lebanon. He knew Lebanon was too weak to want to get involved in a war with Israel, but he wanted his Lebanese flank strong enough to keep Israel from attacking Syria through Lebanon. Also, Asad wanted the Israelis to have to worry about their own defense along the Lebanese border. So he enlisted the support of the fighters of the Palestine Liberation Organization in Lebanon, who were only too happy to join the campaign against Israel.

In the spring and summer of 1973, the secret war preparations began to be more apparent in Syria. A Lebanese newspaper reported Asad was openly hailing the intensifying military exercises of the Syrian armed forces. There were other signs of urgent preparations as well. Syrian workers could be seen digging new wells and trenches. In May, Lebanese newspapers reported that King Hussein of Jordan had distributed to his senior army officers copies of a letter which revealed that several Arab countries were getting ready to attack Israel. That summer the Soviet Union increased its shipments of tanks and missiles to Syria.

The government-controlled press began stirring up the emotions of the people, as Asad and other leading Syrians called for war against the "Zionist enemy." In a speech on August 2 Asad described the Israelis as "invaders who are threatening the entire human race, not only the Arab nations." Then, on September 6, one month before the invasion, the Imam of the Great Mosque in Damascus called for a Muslim holy war against Israel.

While Israeli intelligence was aware of these military preparations, it was not sure what they meant. Most Israelis thought Asad too much of a realist to start a war. They figured the Syrians were only preparing militarily because they were afraid Israel was going to attack them. Moreover, Israeli military leaders concluded that the Egyptian military buildup along the Suez Canal was only a training exercise that had no relationship to the Syrian buildup.

The wily Asad proved himself a master of secrecy and deceit. He made sure the Arab invasion of Israel would come as a complete surprise. As part of his carefully planned program of deception, Asad received the United Nations Secretary-General Kurt Waldheim in Damascus in late August to discuss a peaceful settlement in the Middle East. Asad also cleverly leaked information suggesting the Syrians were dissatisfied with Soviet weapons and were interested in purchasing new weapons from the West.

Asad even went so far as to provoke an air battle with the Israelis that cost the Syrian air force thirteen planes. The purpose of the battle was to reveal Israel's aggressive intentions. It then gave Asad the excuse he needed to build up his armed forces on the Golan Heights under the pretext of defending Syria against a possible Israeli offensive.

Israel's battle-hardened defense minister, Moshe Dayan, did not believe the Egyptians would risk crossing the Suez Canal to attack Israeli positions. But he began to suspect that Asad might be bold enough to launch an attack on the Golan Heights. On October 5, the day before the Arab invasion, Dayan ordered reinforcements for his troops on the Golan front and put Israeli armed forces on the highest state of alert. Prime Minister Golda Meir decided that the crisis should be discussed at the next full meeting of the cabinet on October 7. This was the day after Yom Kippur, a day of prayer and fasting which is the holiest day of the Jewish year. That was one day too late. Sadat and Asad had purposely scheduled the invasion for Yom Kippur to catch the Israelis off guard.

AN ATTACK IS LAUNCHED

Early in the morning on October 6, the day set for the surprise attack, Asad waited in the underground war room at army headquarters in Damascus. He waited to give the order to fire Syria's heavy guns against the Israeli positions along the entire Golan front. This was the battle Asad had dreamed of ever since his crushing defeat by the Israelis six years earlier. Asad was so involved in the magnitude of the day that he forgot October 6 was special for another reason. Later, when someone reminded him it was his birthday (he was 43), he said, "You're right. I hadn't noticed."

At the appointed hour Egypt and Syria simultaneously hit the Israelis with full force on both fronts. On the Golan Heights, Syria attacked with 35,000 troops and 800 tanks, breaking through the Israeli defenses in several places. Advance units of the Syrian army approached the eastern shore of the Sea of Galilee, where they were within striking distance of northern Israel. Asad felt he was on the brink of recapturing all of the Golan Heights territory he had lost in the 1967 war.

Egypt also caught Israel by surprise. Along the Suez Canal 4,000 guns and 250 aircraft pounded Israeli positions. The thousands of soldiers the Egyptians ferried across the canal in rubber dinghies overwhelmed Israeli forts and established five defensive positions on the eastern side of the canal. This allowed the Egyptians to build bridges across the canal. The bridges allowed them to transport more than 1,000 tanks and the rest of their 100,000-man attack force to the other side. The Egyptian surge overwhelmed the under-manned Israeli defenses. In early battles the Israelis lost 300 tanks. Then, when the Israelis rushed reinforcements to the front to count-erattack, they lost 260 more tanks.

These Arab attacks caught the Israelis completely by surprise. On the most holy day of the Jewish year Israeli army reservists were caught at prayer or relaxing at home with their families. Hurriedly they had to gather up their gear and rush off to join their units on their way to the two fronts where the Syrians and Egyptians were driving the Israelis back decisively.

These early thrusts against the Israelis, who had seemed unbeat-able, made Asad and Sadat instant heroes in the Arab world. Jews and friends of Israel around the world were shocked by the invasion and alarmed by the news of early Arab successes. After living with the shame of the crushing defeats of 1948, 1956, and especially 1967, the Arabs had now suddenly dared to strike boldly at the powerful Israelis. Whatever the outcome of the war, on its very first day Arabs regained a good deal of their self-respect. Although their moment of triumph was to be short-lived, it proved to be one of great satisfaction for Asad and Sadat and for the rest of the Arab world.

THE TIDE TURNS

Much to Asad's distress, however, the Egyptians did not continue their offensive once they crossed the Suez Canal. After they routed the Israeli tank units on the eastern side, they dug in along the canal. Taking up defensive positions, they refused to push forward into the desert to seize the key passes that controlled the east-west routes across the Sinai Peninsula. The Egyptians had no intention of advancing deeper into the desert beyond their missile protection. They were reluctant to expose their troops to the superior firepower of the Israeli air force.

Sadat had his own agenda. His strategy from the beginning had been to attack the Israelis in order to give the peace process a jolt. He had never intended to wage a full-scale war to recover the Sinai Peninsula, which the Israelis had won from the Egyptians in 1967. Not aware of Sadat's plan, Asad pleaded for a week—from October 7 to 14—for him to order an Egyptian offensive against the Israelis. However, with each new day of Egyptian inaction, Asad's disappointment turned to bitterness as Syria took the full brunt of the Israeli counterattack. Since the Egyptian army dug in along the canal refused to attack, the Israelis concentrated on the Golan Heights. They hit the Syrians hard for a week with rockets, missiles, tanks, and planes, driving them back. Speaking later about the reluctance of the Egyptians to mount an offensive on the Sinai front that week, Asad said, "It was the worst disappointment of the war."

By the time Sadat did give in to Asad's pressure, it was too late. On October 14 Sadat finally launched his offensive into the Sinai. By then the Israelis had driven the Syrians back off the Golan land they had captured early in the war and were pushing them back

Syrian trucks destroyed by Israeli aircraft in the 1973 war.

toward Damascus. Nonetheless, a successful Egyptian attack, even at this late date, might have helped save the day for Asad. But that was not to be.

The Israelis stopped the Egyptian offensive and then turned it into a rout. Israeli planes and tanks destroyed 250 of the attacking Egyptian tanks and drove the rest back to the canal. The Israelis then boldly crossed the canal and attacked the Egyptian army from behind. By October 22 the Israelis had 45,000 Egyptian troops trapped. With the main Egyptian fighting force threatened with extinction and with the Israelis fighting their way ever closer toward Damascus, Asad's dream of liberating the Golan Heights and changing the balance of power in the Middle East was crushed.

The United States and the Soviet Union arranged a cease-fire, which the Security Council of the United Nations adopted as Resolution 338. Egypt and Israel accepted right away, but Asad refused.

He was angry both at Sadat for negotiating with U.S. Secretary of State Henry Kissinger against his wishes and at the United States and the Soviet Union for arranging the cease-fire without consulting him.

However, with Israeli guns only 20 miles from Damascus, Asad could not stand alone for long. So late on October 23, Asad finally agreed to a cease-fire with Israel in order to save his army from further destruction and prevent a complete defeat.

Cease-fire or no cease-fire, Asad did not abandon his struggle against Israel. In December 1973, Egypt, Jordan, Israel, the United States, and the Soviet Union attended a peace conference in Geneva, but Asad stubbornly refused to attend. He stood up to Soviet, American, and Egyptian pressures to take part in the conference. Asad preferred to continue his war against the Israelis along the cease-fire line. Later, when Kissinger became the chief negotiator of the post-war agreements between Israel and Egypt and Syria, Asad took a hard line. He demanded that Israel give up all the territory it captured in the 1973 war and most of what it captured in the 1967 war as well.

Asad was forced to scale down his demands after Sadat reached his own separate agreement with Israel. Since Sadat had not bothered to coordinate his plans with Asad, Asad had to work out his own separate agreement with the Israelis through Kissinger. For five months Asad conducted grueling talks with Kissinger, who called Asad a "proud, tough, shrewd" negotiator. At the same time, Asad continued his deadly border war against the Israelis along the cease-fire line.

Although Asad finally had to settle for less than he demanded, he did succeed in getting the Israelis to withdraw from all the territory on the Golan Heights it had captured in the 1973 war. Asad even got Israel to return the city of Quneitra, which it captured in 1967. Asad's prestige and popularity with the Syrians soared when they learned about the return of Quneitra. He celebrated the "victory" by personally going to the destroyed city and raising the Syrian flag.

After the 1973 war Asad felt frustrated that he could not keep Sadat from making his own separate agreements with Israel. In 1974, when Sadat and Kissinger negotiated a second Egyptian-Israeli Sinai agreement, Asad denounced it as "a total submission to Israeli demands" and "a breach in Arab solidarity." While Sadat moved toward his own separate peace with Israel, Asad stood tough against any compromise with the Israelis. As the Cairo-Damascus Arab alliance that had planned and waged the war fell apart, Asad became the leader of the Arab struggle against Israel.

INVOLVEMENT
IN
LEBANON

ebanon had always been part of Syria until the French made it into a separate province, which then became a separate country in 1945. Like other Syrian nationalists who never accepted the separation, Asad viewed Lebanon as part of Syria, as it had been for many centuries before French rule. Part of Syria's water supply came from Lebanon, and much of Syria's exports and imports passed through the port of Beirut. Many Syrians went to Lebanon to work and then sent money back to their families in Syria. After Syria won its independence from France, Syria refused to establish diplomatic relations with Lebanon because that would have signified acceptance of Lebanon as a separate country.

Asad wanted to control Lebanon for several reasons. He wanted to get rid of or at least control Syrians in Lebanon who opposed his government. Since Lebanon was a democracy, political dissidents and survivors of Syrian political coups often fled to Beirut. There they criticized Asad's government or plotted to overthrow it. Asad also wanted to control the PLO groups that transferred their headquarters and bases to Lebanon after King Hussein drove them out of Jordan in late 1970. Asad needed the PLO and other Lebanese militias as a buffer against the Israelis who could attack Syria through Lebanon. He also needed the PLO fighters in Lebanon to keep up their pressure on Israel with raids across the border.

ASAD SUPPORTS THE LEBANESE GOVERNMENT

Asad spent the early 1970s trying to improve his relations with the Christian-dominated government of Lebanon. In doing so he adopted a policy that was the direct opposite of those who had ruled Syria before him. Syria's earlier rulers had sided with Muslim radicals against pro-Western Christians who controlled the Lebanese government. But Asad decided it was in his interests to befriend the Christians. Asad's family had known Lebanese President Franjiyya and his family, and Asad's brother Rifat was a close personal friend of the president's son.

In cultivating the government, Asad was careful not to antagonize the Lebanese by declaring the historic Syrian claim to Lebanon. Instead, he affirmed the close relationship between the two countries. "There exist special historical relations between Lebanon and Syria and no regime in Syria or in Lebanon can overlook this," he said. "Syria and Lebanon are one land [not one state] and their peoples are more than brothers."

Asad also reached out to groups excluded from the Christian-dominated government, most notably the Shiite Muslims, who were the largest group in Lebanon. Asad established close ties with their powerful leader, Imam Musa al-Sadr. It was Sadr who helped Asad establish his Muslim legitimacy in Syria by declaring that the

Alawites were part of the Shiite branch of Islam. That declaration strengthened Asad against his Muslim critics and helped him win the support of Shiite Muslims in Lebanon. Asad also assisted the PLO in Lebanon by giving them arms and helping them build a military stronghold near the Israeli border.

When Asad visited Beirut in January 1975, the Lebanese government and public received him warmly. After his talks with the president, Asad pledged to support Lebanon's defense of its borders against the threat of Israeli attack. The two leaders also signed an agreement that Syria would send troops to Lebanon to help train the Lebanese army. By 1975 Asad had established himself as a powerful influence in Lebanese politics.

CIVIL WAR IN LEBANON

Asad's careful cultivation of both government and anti-government forces began to unravel in 1975. What grew into the Lebanese civil war started when radical Muslims and the PLO grew strong enough to threaten the Christian-dominated government. The Druze leader, Kamal Junblatt, organized radical Muslims into a coalition of armed militias. He then allied his radical Muslim militias with Palestinian fighters in order to overthrow the Christian-dominated government. Christian militias, in turn, acted more aggressively against the Palestinian and radical Muslim forces.

On April 13, 1975, a major clash erupted between Christians and Palestinians in Beirut. Armed battles between Christian forces and Palestinian and radical Muslim forces followed in other parts of Lebanon. When the PLO decided to join the conflict on the side of the Muslim radicals, the civil war intensified.

At first Asad was reluctant to get involved in the fighting. Lebanon was a fragile patchwork of different peoples—Christians, Sunni Muslims, Shiite Muslims, Druzes, Palestinians—living in their separate areas. Asad knew Lebanon was no place to get involved in sectarian fighting. However, when he saw the violence grow and the radical forces threaten the Lebanese government with collapse, he decided to intervene on the side of the government. He joined President Franjiyya in issuing a document that basically preserved the existing political state of affairs. This document favored the Christians. However, Junblatt immediately rejected the document and denounced Asad as "cunning, a genuine Alawite [who] wants to dominate Lebanon to domesticate the Palestinians."

Asad supported the Christians against the Muslim radicals and PLO for several reasons. He wanted to control a united, undivided Lebanon and thought the Christian government had a better chance of holding it together than any other group. Also, because the Christian government needed his support, it would be easier to control. Asad wanted the Lebanese Christians to depend on him rather than on the French or Israelis. Asad also worried that if the Muslim radicals and the PLO gained the upper hand in the civil war, the Israelis would step in on the side of the Christians. An Israeli intervention might cause a permanent partition of Lebanon and endanger Syria on its Lebanese flank.

Asad did not want a victory by the Muslims and PLO that would create a strong radical government in Lebanon. A government headed by Muslim radicals would be harder to manage, since many of the Muslim radicals, especially Junblatt, were critical of Syria and wanted to free Lebanon from its control. Such a radical government could be a threat to the Asad regime by allying itself with Syria's Arab rival, Iraq. In Lebanon Asad preferred a weak Christian government that needed his protection to a radical Muslim government that didn't.

Asad sent Syrian troops to Lebanon to help the government crush its opponents. He also strongly denounced the two main leaders of the radical forces, Kamal Junblatt and Yasir Arafat, head of the PLO. Asad described Junblatt as "an ambitious adventurer and demagogue with a thirst for power and blood" and set out to undermine his attempt to control Lebanon.

Asad's ruthlessness—the side of his character he reveals when

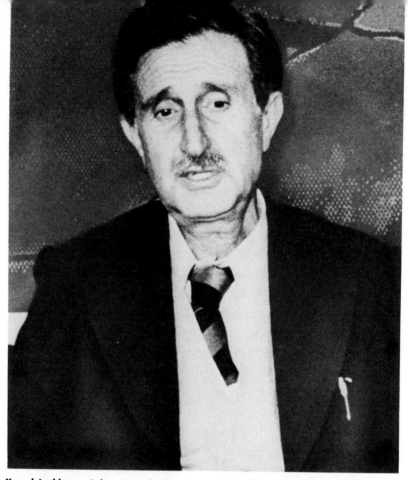

Kamal Junblatt, a Lebanese radical leader, was killed by Asad's forces in 1977.

he feels challenged or threatened—now showed itself. He had his
agents murder Junblatt's sister in May 1976. Although the killer
was never caught, several Lebanese papers denounced the killing as
the work of the Syrians. Then, in March 1977, Asad's agents
assassinated Junblatt himself. Since Junblatt's murder was very
much to Asad's advantage, there was little doubt in anyone's mind
about who had been behind it. Asad was already showing how
ready he was to use violence and terrorism against those who tried
to get in his way.

Asad denounced Yasir Arafat as well. He warned the PLO leader
that he should "stop intervening in domestic Lebanese politics" and
demanded he choose between Junblatt and Syria. When Arafat

chose to remain with Junblatt, Asad sent his army against the PLO. Syrian troops joined Christian forces in attacks on Palestinian refugee camps. In early August 1976, Christian militias laid siege to the large refugee camp of Tal al-Za'tar, killing thousands of Palestinian men, women, and children.

By October, Syrian and Christian troops had defeated the Muslim radicals and Palestinians militarily. That ended the Lebanese civil war, at least for the time being. However, the price of Asad's "victory" was very high. Muslims in Syria and elsewhere in the Arab world were offended that Asad chose to side with the Christians rather than with the Muslims and Palestinians. Many shocked Arabs never forgave him.

ASAD CHANGES SIDES

After his military victory over the PLO in 1976, Asad was unable to bring Arafat and the PLO under his control as he had hoped. Asad became the target of severe criticism throughout the Arab world for his brutal treatment of the PLO. Inside Syria, Muslim fundamentalists stepped up their opposition to his government. Asad began to realize that it was to his advantage to present himself as a defender of Muslim and Palestinian interests rather than as a destroyer. Asad also realized that he needed the help of the PLO against their common enemy, Israel. Asad now tried to make peace with Arafat and the radicals, now led by Kamal Junblatt's son, Walid.

Asad's more peaceful policy toward the PLO and radical Muslims caused Lebanon's Christians to have doubts about him as their protector. Although Asad tried to maintain his close ties with Christian leaders, many of them became suspicious as he became more friendly with their archenemy, the PLO. Christians also began to wonder if Asad ever intended to withdraw his troops from Lebanon. Their suspicions were confirmed when the Arab League endorsed the Syrian troops in Lebanon as a "peace-keeping force."

After Menachem Begin became Israel's new prime minister in 1977, Lebanese Christian contacts with the Israeli government increased. Begin, a hard-line advocate of force against the Arabs, saw the cultivation of ties with Lebanese Christians as a way of increasing Israeli influence in Lebanon. When Israel began supplying the Christian militias with weapons, tensions in Lebanon grew. Asad now shifted his military support from the Christians, increasingly armed and supported by Israel, to the Muslim and Palestinian militias against whom he had fought. The shape of the Lebanese civil war changed dramatically.

Asad's decision to fight *for* the Muslims and Palestinians rather than *against* them was much more acceptable to the rest of the Arab world. Asad's switch also improved his position in Lebanon. Except for the Christian areas and southern Lebanon, where the PLO was in charge, Asad controlled the rest of Lebanon either directly through his own troops or indirectly through the militias of the allies he cultivated and equipped.

THE IRAN FACTOR

In 1979 the revolution in Iran shook the world and changed the shape of politics in the Middle East. In the large and populous nation on the Persian Gulf, the pro-Western government of the shah of Iran was toppled by the Ayatollah Khumeini, the austere and fanatical leader of the Shiite Muslims of Iran. For centuries Shiite Muslims were a persecuted minority in the Middle East. But in Iran, where they were in the majority, they were now in control of the government. Determined to turn Iran into a strict Muslim nation, they called for revolutions throughout the Middle East. Arab governments run by Sunni Muslims quaked in their boots at the prospect of Iranian-style revolutions sweeping across the Arab world.

As usual, Asad was stubbornly himself. He was the only Arab leader to welcome the change, since he saw the fall of the pro-

Western shah as a severe setback to Israeli and American interests in the Middle East. The shah had been a staunch ally of Israel, but with the emergence of the revolutionary regime of the Ayatollah Khumeini, Iran was now Israel's enemy. Unlike other Arab leaders who felt threatened by the Ayatollah's revolution, Asad was an enthusiastic supporter of the new Iranian government.

When the Iran-Iraq war broke out in 1980, Asad offended Arab opinion further by supporting Iran. Iraq attacked Iran to gain control of the disputed Shatt al Arab waterway that formed part of the border between the two countries. In the brutal and bloody conflict that followed, hundreds of men and boys on both sides were sent to their deaths. Asad's support of non-Arab Iran against Arab Iraq put him at odds with Saudi Arabia and the other Persian Gulf states near Iran, as well as with most of the rest of the Arab world. Once more, Asad showed his independent streak by taking a stand that was very unpopular with the rest of the Arabs.

Asad's support for Iran was more than just political. As a man from a rural, poor, minority background, Asad identified strongly with the Iranian Shiites. Since Alawites were linked to the Shiites as one of their offshoots, Asad always felt much closer to Shiite Muslims than to Sunni Muslims, who are in the majority in the Arab world.

The revolution in Iran had a political effect on Lebanon as well. For centuries Shiites in Lebanon had been oppressed and persecuted. They had no voice in Lebanese politics. However, the Shiite revolution in Iran inspired and energized them. When Asad threw his support to Iran in the Iran-Iraq war, he became a hero to Lebanese Shiites. Asad's support for Iran, which offended mainstream Arab opinion, paid rich dividends in Lebanon. The loyalty of Lebanese Shiites created a powerful political link that connected Iran, Syria, and Lebanon. Lebanese Shiite support was to prove a great asset for Asad later against the Israelis when they invaded Lebanon in 1982.

THE WAR
AT HOME

A
fter Asad's armed intervention in Lebanon on the side of
the Christians in the summer of 1976, active Muslim
resistance began inside Syria. In the first few years of his
presidency in the early 1970s, Asad had successfully neutralized
much Muslim opposition to his regime. In response to Muslim
demands, Asad had permitted the addition to his new constitution
of a clause that stipulated that the head of the Syrian state had to be
a Muslim. Then, he had the respected Imam of Shiite Muslims
who lived in Lebanon pronounce the Alawites an authentic Shiite
Muslim community, thus confirming Asad as a true Muslim.

However, after Asad's army intervened in the Lebanese civil war
against Muslims and Palestinians, a general dissatisfaction arose in

Syrian society. By 1976, the economic boom of the early 1970s had leveled off. It created new inequalities that the Baathist revolution had set out to eliminate. A whole new class of profiteers and speculators arose in the upper ranks of the government and military. They grew rich while most Syrians struggled to survive. As Asad's associates and relatives made their fortunes, Asad's popularity decreased.

In an atmosphere of general unrest and Muslim resentment, random bombings and assassinations became more frequent in Syria. These attacks were aimed not only at military officers and Baathist government officials, but also at doctors, teachers, and other professionals, especially if they were Alawites. The campaign, which was mysterious because nobody was sure who was behind it, intimidated Syrian society and terrorized the Alawite community.

In three years—from 1976 to 1979—bombings and assassinations struck down dozens of leading Syrians. The commanders of the missile corps and of the Hama garrison, the director of police affairs at the Ministry of the Interior, and the public prosecutor of the Supreme State Security Court were victims. So were the rector of Damascus University, a professor at Aleppo University, and even Asad's own physician. Asad was shocked and deeply saddened as many of the most promising people in the new Syrian society he was building fell to assassins.

MUSLIM OPPOSITION TO ASAD

Syrian authorities identified the terrorists as members of the Muslim Brotherhood. These were the same Muslim Brothers Asad had battled in the streets in Latakia as a Baathist student leader. The Syrian Muslim Brotherhood was based on the model and teachings of the original Muslim Brotherhood in Egypt. It began in Syria in the late 1930s to protest the French-imposed limitations on the teaching of Islam in Syrian schools.

After independence, the Muslim Brothers opposed the country's new government for trying to weaken Islamic influence in public life. Devout Muslims feared the erosion of traditional Islamic values caused by the increase of European influence on middle- and upper-class Syrians. As the Muslim Brotherhood became stronger, some national politicians sought its support. Some Muslim Brothers were even elected to parliament.

In 1963, when the Baathists came to power and outlawed the Muslim Brotherhood, a fierce conflict erupted between the Muslim Brothers and the new Baathist rulers. From 1963 to 1970 the secular Baathist governments restricted the role of Islam in government and public life. They limited the teaching of Islam in the state schools and reduced the influence of Islamic clerics by cutting back on their duties and income.

The Baathist governments offended wealthy Muslims further with their socialist policies. These policies nationalized industries and large farms and imposed strict government controls on the business activities of the Muslim middle class. These Muslim businessmen in the cities also resented the government for financing development projects in rural and minority areas at the expense of the cities.

Muslims also resented the dramatic rise of the Alawites to power and influence in these Baathist governments. Muslims looked down on Alawites—often servants in middle-class homes—as social inferiors and religious heretics. Muslims also resented the Baathist governments for permitting freer expression in the media, which allowed a wider circulation of Western ideas as well as points of view unfavorable to Islam.

After the Muslim Brothers were outlawed in 1963, they went underground and organized strikes and protests in several Syrian cities against the "godless" government. The government had the Syrian army crack down on the protests and arrested many Muslim religious leaders whom they suspected of stirring up the trouble.

Asad had been able to defuse some of this Muslim resentment

against Baathist rule in the early 1970s. But unhappiness with his Alawite-dominated regime and his intervention in Lebanon on the side of the Christians turned Muslims against Asad in the late 1970s. The Islamic Front, formed in 1980 and representing a broad segment of the Syrian population, published a manifesto of its grievances. It called Asad's regime "a total disaster" and condemned it for suppressing freedom and dissent. According to the manifesto, Asad and his brother Rifat "enslaved the Muslims and stripped them of their wealth, deadened their hearts and spread corruption." Asad's lust for power, it said, "only helped to increase the people's hatred for him."

The public's restlessness and opposition to Asad's regime grew even after Asad changed sides in the Lebanese civil war. Asad's involvement there, which was costing Syria a million dollars a day, was putting an unbearable strain on the economy and causing many hardships for Syrians. Most Syrians were also critical of Asad's support of Iran because it left Syria without friends and allies in the Arab world. Many fundamentalist Muslims in Syria, looking at the successful Islamic revolution in Iran, came to believe they too could overthrow their government.

MUSLIM TERROR INTENSIFIES

In 1979 Muslim extremists increased their strikes against army barracks, police stations, and government and Baath party offices. On June 16 they launched a daring assault on the officer cadet corps of the Aleppo Artillery School. Employing the tactic of surprise, the extremists used machine guns and grenades to kill more than sixty of the cadets as they ate in their dining hall. After the massacre the leaders of the Muslim Brothers proclaimed that their holy war against the government "was now entering a new phase of intensity that would ultimately lead to the fall of Hafiz Asad."

In early 1980 there were violent Muslim uprisings and brutal government repressions in Aleppo and Hama. On June 26 Asad himself barely escaped assassination as he waited to greet an African diplomat on the steps of the government's guest palace. Under cover of machine-gun fire, Muslim extremists penetrated far enough to throw two grenades at Asad. Asad deflected one of them, while one of the guards threw himself on the other and was killed instantly. Asad's personal bodyguard pushed Asad to the ground and covered him with his body as the palace guards cut down the would-be-assassins. Once more Asad barely escaped death.

In the summer of 1980 armed clashes between Muslims and government security forces broke out in several Syrian cities and towns. In December armed Muslims assaulted the government headquarters in Aleppo. The bloody underground war against Asad's government continued throughout 1981. In the spring Muslims staged an open rebellion in Hama and attacked Alawite villages near Latakia. That fall in Damascus a series of car bombs killed many soldiers and civilians and destroyed several government centers.

The extremists had the backing of the Islamic Front, which was attracting broader public support, especially among urban intellectuals and professionals. These intellectuals and professionals had once been supporters of the Baathist government programs in the 1960s and early 1970s. But now they were unhappy with the government and wanted the struggle of the Muslim Brothers against Asad to succeed. By the end of 1981 Syria was on the brink of civil war. Asad had on his hands a nationwide rebellion that threatened the very survival of his regime. Facing his greatest challenge, Asad confided to his Alawite comrades, "It is us or them."

ASAD FIGHTS BACK

Asad fought back against the Muslim threat by trying to divide the Muslim Brothers from the rest of the population. In speeches at Baath party congresses and to the nation over radio and television, Asad portrayed the Muslim Brothers as dangerous fanatics. Government-controlled radio and television denounced them as "criminals," "terrorists," "reactionaries," and "Muslim traitors."

Asad presented himself as a devout Muslim by attending Muslim religious ceremonies in Damascus, sometimes in the company of the chief Muslim cleric. In his speeches he stressed that Islam was a religion of love, justice, and progress, not a religion of hatred, violence, and reaction. Islam was "the greatest revolution in the history of our Arab nation and of humanity." "I believe in God and in the message of Islam," he declared. "I was, I am, and I will remain a Muslim, just as Syria will remain a proud citadel flying high the flag of Islam! But the enemies of Islam who traffic in religion will be swept away!"[1] Asad succeeded in winning to his side important Muslim leaders who denounced the Muslim Brothers as "enemies of Islam."

Asad's public support of the Iranian Revolution and of Iran in the Iran-Iraq war also helped him now in his war against the Muslim Brothers. Iranian leaders wished Asad "success in serving the sacred ideals of the Syrian people" and condemned Asad's enemies inside Syria as "gangs carrying out the Camp David conspiracy [Egyptian-Israeli peace agreement] against Syria in collusion with Egypt, Israel, and the United States."

Asad tried to address himself to popular dissatisfaction with corruption in his government. But nothing seemed to work as corruption in and out of government continued unchecked. The Baath Regional Congress chose Asad's brother Rifat to head up another anticorruption drive in 1979, but Rifat himself was notoriously corrupt. Having risen to the highest level of power in Syrian society on his brother's coattails, Rifat took advantage of his privileged position. He acquired enormous wealth by running a large network of businesses—from operating casinos and nightclubs to smuggling drugs and illegal goods from Lebanon. Corruption reached the highest levels of the military, since Syria's top generals were some of the country's biggest smugglers. One Syrian writer described the situation:

The regime is remote from the people . . . The street is now in a state of corruption—bribery, commission fees, speculation, officers who associate with companies and assist smugglers to take booty from Lebanon. These acts have been committed also by people who are in the government.[2]

Syrians tended to give Asad the benefit of the doubt, thinking of him as honest and well-meaning, even though his government was corrupt. However, by 1980, people wondered how he could permit corruption in his own family. This growing discontent undermined popular support for Asad and his government and increased support for the antigovernment campaign of the Muslim Brothers.

The Muslim Brothers tried to erode Asad's support by using persuasion and intimidation with Alawites to get them to dissociate themselves from him. They warned Alawites not to support Asad and his brother and threatened retaliation against those who did. The 1981 Manifesto of the Islamic Revolution declared: "We hope that the followers of the Alawite sect, to which the people's affliction Hafiz Asad and his butcher playboy brother belong, will positively participate in preventing the tragedy from reaching its sad end."

Asad's brother Rifat had a central role in his brother's war against the Muslim Brothers. Rifat commanded the crack defense forces called on most often to suppress the Muslim resistance. However, the brutality and cruelty that Rifat used against Muslims offended Syrians and only inflamed the Muslim resistance. Soon Asad's government and the Muslim Brothers were caught in a vicious cycle of terror and counterterror. Rifat's troops and other Syrian security forces arrested thousands of suspects, killed hundreds of unarmed civilians, tortured prisoners, and caused suspects to "disappear" without a trace. But nothing the government did seemed to reduce the intensity of the Muslim holy war.

Finally, in late 1980, Asad himself took charge of the war. He

Muslim Brothers, shown here plotting strategy, posed a serious threat to Asad's power in the early 1980s. Asad responded by crushing them in their stronghold of Hama.

ordered all his security forces to attack the enemy with an even more brutal campaign of counterterror measures. These involved indiscriminate arrests, beatings, torture, wholesale destruction of buildings suspected of sheltering opponents, reprisals against the families of the accused, shoot-outs, and mass killings. "It is a sad comedown after the hopes and achievements of his early years," reported one journalist. "Little attempt is made to disguise the fact that this regime is run by and for the Alawite minority."[3]

By the end of 1981 Asad's campaign of brutal suppression and counterterror had succeeded in checking the Muslim rebellion in most of Syria. Only the conservative Muslim city of Hama on the central Syrian plain held out. Long a stubborn opponent of Baathist rule, Hama was the headquarters of the Muslim Brothers and the last stronghold of their rebellion. Muslim discontent in the city and continuing tensions between city authorities and the national government made the city a dangerous powder keg.

THE HAMA MASSACRE

In early 1982, after Asad ordered Rifat to crush this final pocket of Muslim resistance, Rifat sent army troops to Hama. They took up positions outside the city. Then special units entered the city in force to search out the rebel strongholds. On the night of February 2 an army unit in the old city stumbled on the hideout of the local guerrilla commander. Rebel snipers opened fire, killing 20 of the soldiers. When Rifat rushed in more troops, the rebel commander gave the order for a general uprising. Suddenly the lights of all the mosques in the city went on and the loudspeakers the mosques used to call Muslims to prayer called for a holy war against Asad's government.

Hundreds of guerrillas came out of their hiding places and went on a rampage through the city. They burst into the homes of government officials and Baath party workers, captured police stations, and raided armories for more weapons. Determined to take over the city, the rebels surrounded the governor's residence. They fired at his armed guards until government forces were able to fight their way through and rescue the beseiged governor. By morning the guerrillas had massacred seventy leading Baathists. Joyful and confident, the Muslim Brothers declared the city "liberated."

The bloody Hama revolt shocked Asad and his government and filled it with fear, hatred, and a burning desire to revenge the blood of their fallen comrades. Sensing this was the climax of the bitter conflict with the Muslim rebels, Asad decided to wage all-out war. He ordered his best troops and party workers to Hama to crush the uprising and pacify the city. For three weeks the government fought the rebels for control of the city. After 12,000 army troops surrounded Hama and sealed it off, heavily armed units entered the city to hunt down the rebels. The Muslim rebels fought fiercely, but the army's superior firepower forced them back into the old city where they dug in for their battle to the death.

Asad ordered the army to shell the old city mercilessly. He then instructed his generals to send their best troops in to fight the rebels block by block, house by house. The bloody assault demolished entire neighborhoods and killed thousands of innocent people. The army purposely destroyed mosques, churches, museums, and historic monuments and shot entire families. The government killed at least 20,000 people as it destroyed not only the old city, but much of the rest of Hama as well. In the end the Hama massacre broke the back of the Muslim resistance and wiped out the Muslim Brotherhood. It also warned Asad's opponents against further acts of resistance and dissent. By crushing Hama, Asad succeeded in intimidating the Sunni Muslim population of Syria.

The price of Asad's "victory" was high, however. In the early years of his rule Asad had wide popular support. After Hama much of the Syrian population came to fear and hate him. Many thousands of Syrians—mostly business leaders and professionals—fled the country. Inside Syria discontent went underground, where it continues to simmer to this day. All the good things Asad did in the early years of his rule seemed to go down the drain with Hama.

SOURCES—CHAPTER 9

[1]Seale, *Asad*, p. 328
[2]Ma'oz, *Asad*, p. 158
[3]Ma'oz, *Asad*, p. 162

CHAPTER

10

From Defeat To Victory

S oon Asad faced another crisis. The tension between Syria and Israel over Lebanon became so great that it finally exploded in 1982. Since the end of their previous war in 1973, the two countries had been on the brink of war several times over the issue of Syrian missiles in the Biqa Valley and Israeli raids into Lebanon against the PLO. However, the greatest provocation for Asad came on December 14, 1981, when Prime Minister Begin declared that Israel was annexing the Golan Heights. That meant Israel was making the Syrian territory it captured in the 1967 war a permanent part of its territory. Asad was furious, but there was little he could do about it. He was not strong enough to wage war against Israel, and he knew it.

The issue of the PLO bases in Lebanon was what set Begin and Asad on their collision course. Israel regarded the PLO in Lebanon as a threat to its security, since the PLO wanted to drive the Israelis into the sea and create a Palestinian state in place of Israel. The PLO conducted regular guerrilla raids across the border into Israel from their bases in Lebanon. The PLO also committed terrorist acts around the world to draw attention to its cause. Since Asad encouraged and supported the PLO against Israel, Begin knew Israel had to confront Syria as well as the PLO.

In August 1981 Begin made Ariel Sharon, a bold army commander and self-proclaimed enemy of Arabs, his defense minister. Immediately Sharon came up with a secret plan to invade Lebanon in order to strike at both the PLO and Syria. The purpose of the invasion would be to crush the PLO, drive Syrian forces out of Lebanon, and establish a Christian government. The Israeli plan was to install Bashir Jumayyil, the commander of the Christian forces, as president of Lebanon.

By 1982 the stage was set for a clash between Begin and Asad. But the match seemed uneven. Begin had the support of both the Israeli and American public, while in the aftermath of the Hama massacre Asad was hated by large segments of the Syrian people. The Asad government, which had once prided itself on being a "people's democracy," had lost most of its popular support.

Even Asad's power base in the Syrian armed forces was weakening. In early 1982 when Asad uncovered a military plot against his government, he purged more than 100 army officers, including a general and several colonels. Asad's political position in the region also seemed weak. He was on bad terms with King Hussein of Jordan and had yet to bring Lebanon under his control. Even though he supported the PLO and other Palestinian groups at war with Israel, they continued to resist his authority. Nor was Asad able to stop the flow of Israeli weapons to Lebanese Christians.

By contrast, Begin was in a strong position. Egypt was no longer a threat after it signed the Egyptian-Israeli peace treaty that returned the Sinai Peninsula to Egyptian control. Another of Israel's Arab enemies, Iraq, was preoccupied by its war with Iran. Most of all, Begin had the support and protection of the American government, which valued Israel as a close ally and as a democratic bulwark in the Middle East.

THE ISRAELI INVASION OF LEBANON

The spark that set off the Lebanese powder keg came on June 3, 1982. In London, Palestinian gunmen shot and seriously wounded the Israeli ambassador outside his hotel. This terrorist act was the provocation Israel was looking for to launch its invasion. On June 6 Israeli troops poured over the Lebanese border. With a powerful three-pronged thrust they advanced up the coast, into the central mountains, and into the Biqa Valley, where most of the Syrian troops were positioned.

In the first two days of the invasion the Israelis routed the PLO and conquered much of southern Lebanon. They pounded Palestinian refugee camps from land, sea, and air. The Lebanese Christians encouraged attacks against the camps because they wanted to crush the Palestinians and drive them out of Lebanon. World opinion criticized these attacks on the refugee camps, but Begin defended them on the grounds that the camps were training centers for guerrillas and terrorists.

After dispersing the PLO in southern Lebanon, the Israelis turned on the Syrians. On June 9 Israeli planes destroyed Syria's entire SAM missile network in the Biqa Valley. Asad sent his air force up to try to stop the attackers, but it was badly outmatched. The Israelis shot down ninety Syrian planes. The Israeli army pushed into the Biqa Valley and the mountains that surrounded it. Without adequate air cover, the Syrian army was driven back.

Next the Israelis turned their attention to Beirut. The Lebanese capital had once been "the Paris of the Middle East." But already, after seven years of warfare between Christian East Beirut and

Israeli troops in Lebanon during the invasion of 1982.

Muslim West Beirut, the once beautiful city was well on its way to becoming the gutted civil war battlefield it is today. The Israelis tried to get the Christian forces under Bashir Jumayyil to enter Beirut to finish off the PLO, but Jumayyil wanted the Israelis to do the dirty work.

Asad had to stand helplessly by as Israeli planes and guns pounded West Beirut and PLO Chairman Yasir Arafat took center stage as spokesperson for the Arab cause. Fear of heavy casualties and strong criticism of the invasion inside Israel kept Sharon and Begin from ordering the Israeli army into Beirut. To avoid a complete bloodbath and the further destruction of Beirut, the American diplomat Philip Habib tried to persuade the PLO to leave the city.

As the negotiations dragged on through the summer, Sharon unleashed from land, sea, and air salvos of cluster bombs, phosphorus shells, and concussion bombs that brought down entire buildings. During the siege 18,000 Palestinians and Lebanese were killed and more than 30,000 were wounded. The evacuation agreement that Habib finally hammered out in late August resulted in the safe departure from Beirut of more than 10,000 Palestinian fighters and their families as well as 3,600 Syrian troops. With their evacuation, Israel's triumph seemed complete.

LOW POINT

Asad felt humiliated and more alone than ever. He had known defeat before, but never so painfully. In 1967 all Arabs had shared the defeat. In 1973 Asad and Sadat had chosen the time and place for the war and had won early victories that boosted Arab pride. Now in 1982, however, the war had been forced on him and he had to fight Israel alone without help from any other Arab state. For Asad the war was very costly: 1,200 dead, 3,000 wounded, 300 tanks, 140 armored personnel carriers, 80 artillery pieces, and all his SAM missile batteries. Most painful of all for Asad was the loss of more than 90 of his best planes and pilots. To add to the humiliation, Israel lost only one combat jet and one reconnaissance plane.

Only too glad to see Asad disgraced for his support of Iran, other Arab states criticized him and tried to exploit his problems. Both Egypt and Iraq accused him of making a secret deal with Begin to divide up Lebanon. King Hussein of Jordan denounced him for "liquidating the Palestinian cause," while Libya criticized him for having accepted a cease-fire. Asad's patron and arms supplier, the Soviet Union, had remained on the sidelines during the conflict. Asad's only friend had been Iran. Even though it was in the middle of its own bitter war with Iraq, Iran had sent volunteers to the Biqa Valley to fight alongside the Syrians.

To establish Israeli control over Lebanon, Begin wanted the new Christian president of Lebanon, Bashir Jumayyil, to sign a peace treaty with Israel. However, on September 14, 1982, before that could be accomplished, a huge bomb explosion in East Beirut killed Jumayyil and 30 of his associates. Christian troops expressed their outrage with an attack on the Sabra and Shatila refugee camps. More than 1,000 Palestinian men, women, and children were killed in this attack.

Palestinians from the refugee camps of Sabra and Shatila after the 1982 massacre by Lebanese Christian troops.

The massacre of these civilians shocked the world and caused 400,000 Israelis to demonstrate in the streets. Because of Israel's support of the Christian militias, the Israeli protesters demanded an investigation into their country's responsibility for the massacres. It was the largest political demonstration in Israel's history. Yet despite Bashir Jumayyil's death and the Sabra and Shatila massacres, Israel still managed to gain the upper hand in Lebanon. In May 1983 Bashir's older brother, Amin, Lebanon's new president, signed an agreement with Israel that gave Israel ascendency in Lebanon at the expense of Syria.

Another casualty of the 1982 war was a rift between Asad and Yasir Arafat. Arafat was angry that the Syrian army had not come to the rescue of the PLO fighters when Israel invaded Lebanon. The split between the two rivals widened when Arafat showed himself willing to join Jordan in an American-sponsored peace initiative. When Asad discovered that Arafat gave shelter to more than 50 Syrian Muslim radicals who had killed 80 Alawites inside Syria, Asad refused to meet with him anymore. He directed a smear campaign against him in the Syrian media and supported Colonel Abu Musa's revolt against Arafat inside the PLO.

In June 1983 Asad deported Arafat from Damascus and ordered the Syrian army to attack Arafat's PLO loyalists in the Biqa Valley. Arafat and his fighters were forced to flee to Tripoli on the coast of northern Lebanon, but the Syrians forced him to leave Lebanon and set up his headquarters in Tunis, Algeria.

Once more Asad became the object of Arab criticism for his treatment of the PLO. Saudi Arabia and the other Middle Eastern oil-producing states cut off their aid to Syria. Muslim clerics across the Arab world condemned Asad for his hostile actions against the PLO as well as his brutal suppression of Muslims in Syria. The Mufti (chief Muslim cleric) of Jerusalem even called for Asad's death. A group of Iraqi Muslim clerics denounced Asad:

> Hafiz al-Asad, the oppressive tyrant of Syria, bears the blame for the present state of the [Arab] nations' fate...particularly the fate of the Palestinian movement...because of the series of crimes he has committed against the Syrian people, the Palestinian people, and the Iraqi people.[1]

ASAD'S RECOVERY

Asad's most effective weapon against the Israelis turned out to be Lebanese Shiites. At first many of the Shiites in southern Lebanon had welcomed Israel's invasion because it chased the Palestinians away. However, this support faded as the Israeli occupation lengthened and became more oppressive. Israeli support for Christian control of the Lebanese government made the Shiites even more bitter.

The militant Shiite group, Amal, led the fight against the Israeli occupation. Amal had as much religious fervor as the Shiite revolutionaries in Iran with whom Amal had close ties. In fact, Iran sent 2,000 volunteers to help the Lebanese Shiites fight the Israelis, thus forging a strong Lebanese-Iranian Shiite fighting force. These Shiite guerrillas possessed a fanatical willingness to martyr themselves and a burning hatred of Israel and the United States. Willing to undertake suicide missions, the Shiite guerrillas became deadly weapons in Asad's arsenal. His alliance with Iran, which drew so much hostile criticism from other Arabs, now began paying off.

Shiite guerrillas made Israeli army units the targets of snipers, ambushes, booby-trapped cars, and hand-grenades thrown from passing cars. These hit-and-run attacks killed and wounded many Israeli soldiers, lowered the morale of the army, and turned the Israeli public against the occupation. Most Israelis were killed one or two at a time, but there were bigger attacks as well. The most dramatic of these attacks was a huge explosion at the Israeli army staff headquarters in Tyre that killed 67.

After waging its deadly war against its Muslim opponents inside Syria, Asad's powerful security forces now concentrated on supplying, assisting, and directing Shiite and Palestinian guerrillas in Lebanon. Palestinians who had fled the Israeli invasion and sought safety in the Biqa Valley or in Syria itself were only too happy to continue their struggle against the Israelis.

To rebuild his military strength, Asad turned once more to the Soviet Union. He needed to replace his lost weapons, especially the missiles and the aircraft the Israelis destroyed in the summer of 1982. The Soviets obliged. With the arrival of advanced weapon systems from the Soviet Union, Asad began to be more assertive. In the spring of 1983 when the Israelis protested about the installation of advanced SAM-5 missiles, Asad refused to remove them. Having lost more than 500 soldiers to guerrilla attacks, the Israelis were in no mood to go to war with Syria over the missiles.

Asad's new boldness also made him willing to defy the United

States, which was trying to advance a peace plan for the Middle East. He was convinced the American government had encouraged Israel's invasion of Lebanon. He was also offended that the United States helped bring about the Lebanese-Israeli agreement of May 1983 without consulting him about it. Asad regarded the United States as his enemy because it protected Lebanon's Christian government and supported the Israeli occupation.

When the United States tried to pressure Asad to accept the Lebanese government that had signed the accord with Israel, Asad refused. Syrian troops have a right to be in Lebanon, he declared, but Israeli troops do not. His position was that Lebanon and Syria were one land, one people, one nation. In an interview he stated:

> It is a mistake for anyone to believe or think that we will ever leave Lebanon as a morsel which it is easy for the Israelis to swallow because Lebanon is an Arab country to which we are bound by a common history and a common destiny.[2]

As the guerrillas continued their deadly attacks against the Israeli army, the momentum in Lebanon shifted in Asad's favor. Syrian influence increased steadily while that of the Israelis and their Christian allies decreased. In Israel public opinion was divided about the occupation and about the wisdom of the accord the government signed with Lebanon's weak Christian government. Depressed by the ever-mounting Israeli casualties in Lebanon, as well as by his wife's death, Begin shocked the country when he unexpectedly announced his resignation and then secluded himself in his house. In the meantime, the Israeli army in Lebanon kept retreating south toward Israel in the face of constant guerrilla attacks and the hostility of the Shiite population. Finally the Israelis pulled back to a "security zone" near the border that was easier to defend.

The guerrillas also struck at the multinational force of American, French, British, and Italian troops that came to Lebanon to protect the Christian government. On October 23, 1983, a Shiite suicide car bomb attack at the Beirut airport killed 241 American marines. On the same day another car bomb attack killed 56 French soldiers. On December 4 guerrillas killed 8 more marines, while Syrian guns shot down 2 American planes. The guerrilla pressure became so great that the multinational force pulled up stakes and left Lebanon in early 1984.

Without his Western protectors the Lebanese president, Amin Jumayyil, was now at Asad's mercy. With no alternative but to acknowledge Asad's power and seek his support, he traveled to Damascus to pay homage to Asad on February 29, 1984. After he informed Asad he was ready to cancel the accord he had signed with the Israelis, it was formally nullified on March 5, 1984.

Thus, within two years after his humiliating defeat at the hands of the Israelis, Asad was back in his dominant position in Lebanon. Syrian troops were back in force in the Biqa Valley as Asad's Lebanese allies grew stronger by the day. Asad had achieved something no other Arab leader had ever achieved. He proved that Israelis were not invincible and that Arabs were not doomed to defeat and powerlessness. In standing up to his enemies and driving them out of Lebanon, Asad won grudging respect even from critics. His success in Lebanon strengthened his position as a powerful force to be reckoned with in the Middle East.

SOURCES—CHAPTER 10

[1]Ma'oz, *Asad*, p. 168
[2]Seale, *Asad*, p. 413

MORE
CHALLENGES

I n late 1983 Asad had a heart attack. He was struck late at night in his office in the midst of the tense confrontation with Israel and the United States over Lebanon. He was rushed to the hospital and put in the intensive care unit. Doctors treated Asad with powerful sedatives around the clock for two weeks. Then they sent him to a private villa near Damascus for a complete rest. The country wondered what was going on, as even the senior people in Asad's government were not allowed to see him. During his long recovery, rumors circulated that Asad was terminally ill and even that he had been assassinated.

RIFAT'S THREAT

Asad's illness and his long absence from public life created a power vacuum at the center of the Syrian government. Syrian generals who feared that Asad was dying and that his death would throw the country into chaos turned to Asad's brother Rifat. Rifat was the powerful head of the defense forces that helped Asad seize power in 1970 and led the government suppression of the Muslim opposition in the early 1980s.

Rifat was only too glad to receive the attention of the generals and be thought of as the heir apparent. Convinced his older brother was dying, Rifat began acting as if he was already Syria's ruler. He went so far as to press for the resignation of the prime minister and cabinet so that he could put his own supporters in charge of the government. However, as Asad began his recovery, the generals withdrew their support from Rifat and rallied to the ailing president's side.

In the meantime, Asad learned of Rifat's actions and suspected him of planning a coup. Asad ordered the head of his military intelligence to put Rifat and the leaders of his defense forces under surveillance. Asad also ordered his generals to move their units into Damascus to counter Rifat's troops. As the two rival military forces took up positions in Damascus, the country seemed on the verge of civil war. Asad made a brilliant move to defuse the crisis. He appointed Rifat one of the three vice-presidents of Syria and relieved him of his position as commander of the defense forces. What seemed like a promotion was in fact a clever power play that separated his ambitious brother from his power base.

But Rifat refused to give in. By now he was determined to replace his brother, not just wait his turn to succeed him after he died. On March 30, 1984, Rifat ordered his forces to take up key positions around Damascus while his associates put up his picture in public places all around the capital. Army units loyal to Asad confronted Rifat's troops in a series of tense standoffs that threatened to plunge the capital into bloody warfare.

Asad refused to give the order to his troops to fire on Rifat's forces. Instead, Asad chose to confront his brother face-to-face. Taking only his son Basil with him, Asad drove to Rifat's house. Asad had arranged for his mother to travel down from the mountain village of Qurdaha where Asad grew up and where she still lived, knowing she could help Rifat come to his senses. The two brothers argued with each other for over an hour, but in the end Asad's gamble paid off. Rifat agreed to back down from the military showdown.

Nonetheless, Rifat continued to criticize his brother's policies. Rifat wanted Syria to be more Western in its outlook. He was critical of his brother's dependence on the Soviet Union, his alliance with Iran, and his continuing hostility toward Arafat and the PLO. Shocked and hurt by Rifat's disloyalty, Asad reduced his power and influence so much that Rifat finally left Syria. Today Rifat lives comfortably in Paris with his many supporters. He still dreams of ruling Syria after his brother passes from the scene.

LEBANON

Today most of Lebanon accepts Asad's supremacy, although resistance to his control continues, especially in Christian areas. In 1987, thirteen pro-Syrian groups in Lebanon, including Shiites, Sunnis, and Druzes, formed a Unification and Liberation Front, which favored the integration of Lebanon and Syria. However, in the summer of 1988 the plan fell through. Asad was unable to install his choice as Lebanon's new president and the Christian commander of the Lebanese army, General Michel Aoun, defied Asad. When Aoun denounced Syria's "foreign domination" and promised to drive the Syrians out of Lebanon, Asad ordered Syrian guns to pound Christian positions.

Then, in the fall of 1989—after fourteen years of civil war—Lebanese Christian and Muslim representatives met in Saudi Arabia to draw up a charter for power-sharing in Lebanon. The charter called for reunification under a new system of government that recognized the predominance of Muslims—Shiite as well as Sunni—in Lebanon. Under the new arrangement the Muslim majority was to have a greater role in decision-making than it used to when the Christians controlled the government. The charter also accepted Syria's military presence and recognized its leading role in Lebanon.

Shortly after the charter was implemented and a new president, who was Christian, was elected, General Aoun denounced the new charter. Unhappy at the prospect of the loss of Christian power, Aoun vowed to fight the charter even though many Christian legislators and church leaders endorsed it as a fair and sensible arrangement. By 1990 Christian factions, deeply divided about the charter and its new government, fought bitterly against each other in the main Christian area of Lebanon. Nonetheless, despite this Christian opposition, the charter was a victory for Asad. Supported by most Lebanese, it seeks to put badly divided Lebanon back together again in the shadow of his power and influence.

TERRORISM

From the beginning Asad has shown his willingness to use terrorism—assassination, sabotage, intimidation, guerrilla warfare—to fight his enemies and achieve his goals. While he was Syria's defense minister in the late 1960s and after he came to power in 1970, Asad supported Palestinian guerrilla raids from Syrian territory against civilian targets inside Israel. Then, after he became involved in the Lebanese civil war, he had his agents murder Kamal Junblatt and his sister. At home Asad met the terrorism of the Muslim Brothers with a ferocious counterterror of his own. Asad routinely hunted down his enemies abroad as well. In

1980 Syrian agents in Paris assassinated Salah al-Din Bitar, one of the founders of the Baath party. In 1981 Syrian agents in Aachen, West Germany, intending to assassinate one of the leaders of the Syrian Muslim Brothers, murdered his wife instead.

Asad's most successful use of terrorism had been in Lebanon, where his agents directed operations against his enemies—the Israelis, Americans, Lebanese Christians, and Arafat's PLO. The chief of Syrian intelligence in Lebanon coordinated the campaign, which was carried out mostly by Asad's allies—Lebanese Shiites, Syrian-based Palestinians, and the fanatic Iranian Islamic Jihad group sent by the Khumeini government. The major successes of this terrorist campaign were the assassination of Lebanon's president, Bashir Jumayyil, in 1982; the suicide attack on the U.S. Marine compound, which killed 241 marines in 1983; the blowing up of the U.S. embassy in Beirut in 1984; and the long series of guerrilla and suicide attacks against the Israeli army in Lebanon in 1983–84.

The success of the campaign encouraged Asad to continue operations against Israeli and American targets abroad. On December 27, 1985, gunmen from Abu Nidal's organization, which was based in Syria, shocked the world by attacking civilians at the Rome and Vienna airports on the same day, killing 20 people and wounding 110. On April 2, 1986, a bomb planted on a TWA airliner flying over Greece exploded and killed 4 Americans. Two weeks later a terrorist tried to place a bomb on an Israeli airliner carrying close to 400 passengers. But he failed.

In May 1986 the director of America's Central Intelligence Agency, William Casey, stated:

> Libya, Syria, and Iran use terrorism as an instrument of power. They hire and support established terrorist organizations....Syria traditionally has regarded terrorism as a weapon to be used in precisely defined and calculated ways to war against Israel and to intimidate or eliminate forces resisting Syrian President Hafiz Asad's drive to make Syria the dominant force in the Arab world.[1]

President Asad of Syria greets President Qadhafi of Libya at an Arab summit meeting in 1989. Both leaders have supported terrorism to advance their goals.

Asad denied his involvement in international terrorism, but there was too much evidence that linked Syria to a global network of terrorism. Syria's support of terrorism prompted Britain to break off diplomatic relations with Syria in 1986. Later the United States, Canada, Italy, and West Germany did the same. In the late 1980s the United States and several Western European countries imposed economic sanctions on Syria to protest Asad's links to international terrorism.

NEW DEVELOPMENTS

In the late 1980s Asad took steps to shed his reputation as a terrorist and repair his relations with the West. In February 1987 Asad sent 7,000 Syrian troops into West Beirut to curb Hizballah, the Iranian-backed Shiite fundamentalist group that was kidnapping Americans and Europeans. In July 1987 he closed the Damascus offices of Abu Nidal and expelled his terrorist organization from Syria. These signs that Asad was beginning to curb his support for terrorism, at least in its more extreme form, prompted several Western nations to resume relations with Syria and lift their economic sanctions.

At the end of the 1980s Asad had to adjust to new international developments. His biggest challenge involved the dramatic changes that were sweeping through the Soviet Union and Eastern Europe. Poland, Czechoslovakia, and Hungary held elections and voted in new governments committed to democracy and freedom. East Germany dropped its communist system and chose to unite with West Germany. President Gorbachev's reforms in the Soviet Union changed his country's foreign policy as well. The Soviets pulled their troops out of Afghanistan and adopted a much more friendly policy toward the United States and Europe.

In the Middle East these changes had important consequences. Palestinians and Arab states like Syria no longer could count on training and weapons from Eastern-bloc countries, as these countries established relations with Israel and reached out to Western Europe and the United States for more trade and better relations. The Soviet Union, Syria's main arms supplier for three decades, told Asad it would no longer support his military buildup or supply him with weapons against Israel. By 1990 Arabs were no longer in a position to play the Cold War superpowers off against each other.

The end of the Iran-Iraq war in 1989 created another problem for Asad. Through the 1980s the war had kept Asad's rival, President Saddam Hussein of Iraq, preoccupied. After the war ended, Hussein showed signs of wanting to get even with Asad for his support of Iran. Hussein sent Iraqi weapons to General Aoun in Lebanon to encourage him to continue his defiance of Syria. To protect himself against the Iraqi threat, Asad drew closer to Egypt, the country he had shunned because it made peace with Israel. Asad made more peaceful overtures to the West as well.

In March 1990, when former American president Jimmy Carter visited Asad in Damascus, Carter came away from their meeting convinced that Asad was adopting a more peaceful approach. Asad expressed willingness to hold direct peace talks with Israel at an international conference on Middle Eastern peace. Carter also reported that Asad wanted to help gain the release of the hostages held in Lebanon. He told Carter Syrian officials would try "to both locate the hostages and convince those who might be holding them they should be protected and released." When two American hostages—Robert Polhill and Frank Reed—were subsequently released via Damascus, Asad was given part of the credit.

SOURCE—CHAPTER 11
¹Ma'oz, *Asad*, p. 175

Epilogue

I n the last two decades under President Asad, Syria has made great progress. At the time of its independence it had been weak, divided, and backward, but since that time Syria has become a strong, highly centralized nation that Asad has made a powerful force in the Middle East.

Although Asad has never been able to defeat Israel in war, Syria is now stronger than ever. Asad modernized his army of 500,000 regulars with new Soviet weapons and improved his air force sufficiently to challenge Israel's air superiority. Asad has also installed a powerful antiaircraft system and has equipped his forces with long-range ground-to-ground missiles and chemical weapons. Even though Israel still has the military advantage, Syria is now strong enough to defend itself against Israel. "The Israelis are aware that their next war will by no means be a limited war, nor would it be a picnic," explains Syria's foreign minister. "They are also aware of the heavy losses that they would suffer."

Despite this military buildup, however, Asad has not been able to win back the Golan Heights from Israel either by war or by negotiations. Although he was unable to stop President Sadat of Egypt from making his own separate peace with Israel, he has been able to foil the peace moves of other Arabs. In 1984 he pressured the Lebanese president to abandon the Israeli-Lebanese accord, and so far he has blocked Jordan and the PLO from engaging in peace talks with Israel.

Asad is also winning the battle for Lebanon. With the help of his Lebanese allies and 40,000 Syrian troops, Asad now controls two-thirds of Lebanon. Although pockets of resistance to his position as Lebanon's unofficial ruler continue, Asad definitely has the upper hand.

At home, Asad deserves credit for advancing the Baathist social revolution. A lifetime member of the Baath party and a firm believer in its principles, Asad has continued the party program that reduced the privileges of the wealthy upper class and improved the fortunes of Syrian peasants, workers, and minorities. Education is now available at all levels of Syrian society, and government power projects supply electricity to the most remote corners of the country. Asad's industrialization program has increased employment, improved communications and technology, and raised Syria's standard of living.

Asad has had his failures, too. Waste, inefficiency, and corruption plague government and business. Agriculture production is lagging, making fruits and vegetables harder to obtain. Also, high inflation rates continue to erode the earning power of Syrian workers. During the first six years of Asad's rule, Syria experienced impressive economic growth. But beginning in 1976 with Asad's economically draining involvement in Lebanon, the boom faded and Syria began facing one serious economic problem after another. Most distressing for many Syrians has been the emergence of a new privileged class. Senior military officers and high government and party officials take advantage of their positions to get rich. They live high off corruption while most Syrians struggle to make a living.

Asad's record on human rights is terrible. In recent years Asad has improved his image as a sponsor of international terrorism, but inside Syria Asad has shown no sign of softening his regime's brutal repression. Syrians are not allowed to express their opposition to the government. They can complain in private, but they do not have the right to criticize Asad or his government in public. If they do, Asad's security forces will quickly silence them. These secret police have an elaborate intelligence network that reaches out into every corner of Syrian life.

The thousands of political prisoners who fill the prisons of Syria are tortured regularly. Asad's security forces even arrest the prisoner's relatives and torture them, too. The human rights organization, Amnesty International, issued a detailed report on Syrian human rights abuses in 1987. Based on the testimony of numerous victims, the report documented no fewer than thirty-eight different methods of torture security forces use on prisoners. Many of these tortures are carried out in special prison torture chambers. By the early 1990s there was no evidence that President Asad was doing anything to improve his human rights record.

Asad is now much more isolated than he was at the beginning of his rule. In his first years in power he sought wide popular support and took steps to make Syrians feel included in his government. But by 1976 disillusionment began setting in. Sunni Muslim alienation, widespread corruption, severe economic problems, human rights violations, and a general dislike of Alawites have all contributed to the resentment large segments of the Syrian population feel toward Asad and his government. Asad's base of support has narrowed so much that today most Syrians regard his regime as little more than an Alawite military dictatorship.

How long will Asad hang on? Who will succeed him? How will Syria fare after he leaves the scene? These are questions yet to be answered. Asad is now in his early sixties. Although he seems fully recovered from his heart attack, those who saw Asad after his convalescence reported that he looked at least ten years older. Although he looks thinner and less robust and rumors continue to circulate about his poor health, Asad has looked healthy enough in his recent public appearances.

The former American Secretary of State Henry Kissinger once called Asad "the most interesting man in the Middle East." Asad may also be the most cunning, judging from the length of time he has survived in power in the Middle Eastern world of tribal feuds, political assassinations, sectarian violence, revolutionary ferment, and fierce religious passions. Indeed, that may prove to be Asad's greatest accomplishment of all—that he fought his way to power and remained there for more than twenty years. In the dangerous world of Middle Eastern politics that is no small accomplishment.

TIME LINE

ca. 2100 B.C.	Amorites settle in the area which is to become Syria
11th–6th century B.C.	Assyrians rule Syria
6th–4th century B.C.	Syria is part of the Persian Empire
333–331 B.C.	Alexander the Great conquers Syria
63 B.C.	Roman rule of Syria begins
A.D. 633–640	Syria conquered by Arab armies; most Syrians are converted to Islam
661–750	Umayyad caliphs in Damascus rule the Arab world
11th–14th century	Europeans come to Syria on Crusades
1516–1918	Syria is part of the Ottoman Turkish Empire
1914–1918	World War I
1920	Syria becomes part of a French mandate
1930	*Hafiz al-Asad is born in the village of Qurdaha*
1939	*Asad attends school in Latakia for a year;* World War II breaks out in Europe
1945	World War II ends; *Asad begins secondary school in Latakia*
1946	Syria achieves its independence; *Asad joins the Baath Party*
1948	Syria and other Arab states declare war on Israel
1949	First military coup in Syria
1951	*Asad graduates from secondary school and enrolls in the pilot training school at Aleppo*
1955	*Asad becomes an officer in the Syrian air force*

1956	President Nasser of Egypt nationalizes the Suez Canal
1958	Syria and Egypt join together in the United Arab Republic (UAR); *Asad marries Aniseh Makhlaf*
1961	New Syrian government secedes from the UAR
1963	Baathists seize control of the Syrian government
1964	*Asad is made commander of the Syrian air force*
1966	*Asad becomes Minister of Defense as a result of a coup by radical Baathists*
1967	War between Israel and the Arab states; Syrian air force is destroyed; the Golan Heights is lost to Israel
1970	*Asad seizes control of the Syrian government*
1971	*Asad takes on the position of President of Syria*
1973	Syrians endorse a new constitution; Syria and Egypt wage war against Israel
1975	Civil war breaks out in Lebanon as Christians and Palestinians clash in Beirut
1979	Revolution in Iran overthrows the shah and brings Islamic fundamentalists to power
1980	War breaks out between Iran and Iraq; the Islamic Front is established and condemns Asad's regime
1980–1981	*Muslim extremists attempt to kill Asad; Syria is on the brink of civil war as the Muslim Brothers oppose Asad's government*
1982	*Asad puts down an uprising by the Muslim Brothers in a bloody massacre at Hama;* Israeli troops invade Lebanon
1983	Lebanon's president gives Israel a free hand in Lebanon at the expense of Syria; *Asad suffers a near-fatal heart attack*

1984	Multinational peace-keeping forces withdraw from Lebanon after suffering terrorist attacks by Shiite guerrillas; *Asad and his brother fight for control of Syria's government*
1989	Christians and Muslims draw up a charter for power-sharing in Lebanon; Iran-Iraq war ends
1990	*Asad turns sixty; he helps gain the release of two American hostages held in Lebanon;* Iraq invades Kuwait

GLOSSARY

Alawites (Al uh weets)   A Syrian religious minority. Alawites live in the Alawi mountains in western Syria. Asad is an Alawite.

Arafat, Yasir (AHR uh fat, YAHseer)   Chairman of the Palestine Liberation Organization (PLO).

Asad, Hafiz al- (ah SAHD, HAH fehz uhl)   President of Syria since 1971.

Asad, Rifat al- (ah SAHD, REE faht uhl)   Asad's younger brother. Rifat once headed the Defense Forces that protected Asad and his regime. After he fell out of favor with his brother, Rifat moved to Paris.

Baath party (BAH ath)   A political party that believes in the rebirth of Arab culture and values. Asad joined the Baath party at the age of 16.

Begin, Menachem (BAY guhn, mehn AHK kehm)   The Israeli prime minister from 1977 to 1983. The bitter rivalry between Begin and Asad exploded when the Israelis invaded Lebanon in 1982.

Beirut (bay ROOT)   The capital of Lebanon.

Biqa Valley (BIH kah)   A valley in eastern Lebanon controlled by Syria.

Cold War   The intense political and military rivalry between the United States and the Soviet Union. The Cold War began after World War II and lasted for four decades.

coup (koo)   A sudden overthrow of a government by a small group of conspirators.

Damascus (duh MAS kuhs)   The capital of Syria.

Druzes (DROOZ ehz)   A religious sect. In Syria, the Druzes live in the Druze mountains in the southern part of the country.

Golan Heights (GOH lahn)   The part of southern Syria the Israelis captured in the 1967 war.

Hama (HAH mah)   The Syrian city where Asad's government crushed a Muslim uprising in 1982.

Hussein, King (hoo SAYN)   The ruler of Jordan since 1953.

Hussein, Saddam (hoo SAYN, SAH dahm)   President of Iraq.

Islam (IHS luhm)   The religion of Muslims, who believe Allah is God and Muhammad is his prophet.

Ismailis (is MAY leez)   A sect of Shiite Muslims.

Jadid, Salah (jah DEED, SA lah)   One of the original members of the Military Committee. He, Umran, and Asad seized power in 1963. In 1966 he and Asad ousted Umran, and he in turn was ousted by Asad in 1970. Asad put Jadid in a Damascus prison, where he remains to this day.

Khumeini, Ayatollah (koh MAY nee, eye uh TOH luh) Iranian Shiite religious leader who led the revolution that overthrew the Shah of Iran in 1979.

Latakia (LAT uh KEE uh) Syrian coastal city where Asad attended secondary school.

mandate (MAN dayt) A commission to rule granted by the League of Nations. After World War I (1914-1918) the League of Nations gave France a mandate to rule Syria.

Military Committee A group of five young Syrian Baathist officers. While stationed in Cairo, they met secretly to discuss politics and Syria's future. The Military Committee organized the coup that brought the Baathists to power in 1963. Asad was one of its founding members.

Muslim Brotherhood (MUHZ luhm) An organization of Muslim fundamentalists that resisted Asad's government.

Muslims Followers of Islam who believe Allah is God and Muhammad is his prophet.

Nasser, Gamal Abdel (NAH sehr, gah MAHL AHB duhl) Former president of Egypt. Nasser was the leading Arab spokesperson in the 1950s and 1960s.

National Progressive Front A group of Syrian political parties closely allied with the governing Baathist party.

Palestine Liberation Organization (PLO) The largest Palestinian group. Headed by Yasir Arafat, the PLO is a political and military organization that seeks to establish a Palestinian state.

Quneitra (KU nay truh) Syrian city on the Golan Heights. The Israelis captured Quneitra in the 1967 war but returned it to Syria after the 1973 war.

Qurdaha (cur DAH hah)   The Alawite village in which Asad's family lived for generations. Asad was born and raised in Qurdaha.

Sadat, Anwar (suh DAHT, AHN wahr)   Former president of Egypt. Sadat joined Asad in the 1973 war against Israel, but later he made a separate peace with Israel. Sadat was assassinated in 1981.

Saladin (SAL uh dihn)   Muslim warrior-hero of the Middle Ages. Saladin defeated the European Crusaders and helped drive them out of the Middle East.

sect (sekt)   An offshoot of a larger religious group.

Shiites (SHEE eyets)   Members of one of the two main branches of Islam. Shiite Muslims are outnumbered by Sunni Muslims in the Arab world, but they are the majority in Iran, where they seized control of the government in 1979.

Sunnis (SOON eez)   Members of the majority branch of Islam.

terrorism (TER uh riz uhm)   The use of assassination, sabotage, kidnapping, airplane highjackings, and other violent acts to achieve political goals.

Umayyads (oh MY ads)   An Arab dynasty. Umayyad caliphs in Damascus ruled the Arab world from A.D. 661 to 750.

Umran, Muhammad (UM rahn, moh HAM uhd)   One of the original members of the Military Committee. After the 1963 coup, Umran, Jadid, and Asad ran the government. Umran was ousted by Jadid and Asad in 1966 and later assassinated in Lebanon.

United Arab Republic (UAR)   The union of Egypt and Syria that lasted from 1958 to 1961.

BIBLIOGRAPHY

Books

The Cambridge Encyclopedia of the Middle East and North Africa. Cambridge: Cambridge University Press, 1988.

Devlin, John. *Syria: Modern State in an Ancient Land.* Boulder, CO: Westview Press, 1983.

Friedman, Thomas L. *From Beirut to Jerusalem.* New York: Farrar, Straus & Giroux, 1989.

Gordon, Matthew S. *Hafez Al-Assad.* New York: Chelsea House, 1990.

Khadduri, Majid. *Arab Personalities in Politics.* Washington, DC: The Middle East Institute, 1981.

Ma'oz, Moshe. *Asad: The Sphinx of Damascus*. New York: Weidenfeld & Nicolson, 1988.

The Middle East (6th edition). Washington, DC: Congressional Quarterly, 1986.

Seale, Patrick. *Asad: The Struggle for the Middle East*. Berkeley: University of California Press, 1989.

Syria: Torture by the Security Forces. New York: Amnesty International Publications, 1987.

van Dam, Nikolaos. *The Struggle for Power in Syria*. New York: St. Martin's Press, 1979.

Periodicals

Cowell, Alan, "Trouble in Damascus," *New York Times Magazine*, April 1, 1990.

Rabinovich, Itamar, "Is Syria Declining as a Power?" *New York Times*, August 17, 1989.

Viorst, Milton, "Letter from Damascus," *The New Yorker*, January 8, 1990.

INDEX

Gorbachev, President, 108
Great Britain, 12, 37, 38

Habib, Philip, 95
Hafiz, Amin al-, 47, 48, 49–51,
  58–59
Hama (Syria), 8, 85, 86, 90–91,
  93, 118
Hixballah (fundamentalist group),
  107
Homs (Syria), 8, 60
Homs military academy, 35, 42
Hostages, 109
Human rights, 112
Hungary, 108
Hussein, King, 66, 67, 75, 93,
  96, 118
Hussein, Saddam, 108, 118

Iran, 80–81, 85, 87, 94, 96, 99,
  104, 106, 108
Iraq, 46, 58, 65, 77, 81, 87, 96,
  98, 108
Islam, 11, 31, 57, 83, 84, 86, 118
  see also Muslims
Islamic Front, 85, 86
Islamic Jihad, 106
Ismailis, 13, 42, 118
Israeli-Arab conflict see Arab-
  Israeli conflict
Italy, 107

Jadid, Salah, 46, 48, 49–51, 53,
  54, 59, 61, 118
Jordan, 51–52, 65, 66, 67, 72, 75,
  96, 98, 111
Jumayyil, Amin, 97, 101
Jumayyil, Bashir, 93, 95, 96, 106
Junblatt, Kamal, 76, 77, 78, 105
Junblatt, Walid, 79

Khaddam, Abd al-Halim, 61
Khumeini, Ayatollah, 80, 81, 106,
  119
Kissinger, Henry, 72, 73, 113

Latakia (Syria), 23–24, 26–27,
  29–33, 83, 86, 119
League of Nations, 12, 119
Lebanon, 13, 44, 66–67, 74–82,
  85, 92–101, 104–106, 109, 111
Libya, 60, 96, 106
Local government, 60–61

Mandate, definition of, 119
Manifesto of the Islamic
  Revolution, 88
Medicine, 33
Meir, Golda, 68
Mezze air base, 36
Military Committee, 42–51, 59,
  119
Missiles, 92, 94, 96, 99
Muhammad, 11, 13–14
Munira (cousin), 21
Musa, Abu, 98
Muslim Brotherhood, 31–32,
  83–90, 105, 119
Muslims, 76–80, 82–91, 98, 99
  see also Shiite Muslims;
  sunni Muslims

Nasser, Gamal Abdel, 37, 41–43,
  45, 47, 119
National Progressive Front, 59,
  60, 119
Nidal, Abu, 106, 108
Nixon, Richard, 7

Ottoman Turkish Empire, 11–12

Palestine Liberation Organization
  (PLO), 66, 75–80, 92–95,
  97–98, 104, 111, 119
Palestinians, 76–80, 82, 94, 99,
  105, 106
People's Assembly, 56–57, 60
PLO see Palestine Liberation
  Organization
Polhill, Robert, 109
Poland, 108
Provisional Regional Command,
  58

ABOUT
THE AUTHOR

Charles Patterson grew up in New Britain, Connecticut, and attended Amherst College and Columbia University, where he earned his Ph.D. Now a writer and editor in New York, he is a member of the Authors Guild, PEN, and the National Writers Union. His previous books are *Anti-Semitism: The Road to the Holocaust and Beyond, Thomas Jefferson,* and *Marian Anderson* (winner of the 1989 Carter G. Woodson Book Award).

Photo Acknowledgments

AP/Wide World Photos: pp. 10, 23, 50, 56, 65, 78, 95, 107; Courtesy of the Embassy of the Syrian Arab Republic: pp. 15, 16, 20, 30, 36; Gamma-Liaison: p. 97; North Wind Picture Archives: p. 12; Spengler/Sygma: p. 89; Topham/The Image Works: p. 52; UPI/Bettmann: pp. 39, 71.